# THE AMAZING ADVENTURES OF AN AMISH STRIPPER

## AN EROTIC MEMOIR

### NAOMI SWARTZENTRUBER

Print ISBN: 979-8-9882632-0-3

Ebook ISBN  979-8-9882632-1-0


First Edition 2023

Printed in the United States of America.

Coaching, editing and writing services provided by
M. Maeve Eagan at traumainformedwriter.com.

Cover design by TreeHouse Studio

**Disclaimer**

This memoir is based on the true life of Naomi Swartzentruber. In order to protect the privacy of certain individuals, some names and identifying facts have been changed. The depictions of events as well as verifiable facts, have been recalled and written accurately to the best of the author's ability. This book's descriptions are solely from her own lived experience and do not describe any other person's story or experience. Dialogue and other details may have been changed, added, or withheld. Any supposed likeness to any other persons, communities, or specific locations is unintentional. This memoir was reconstructed based on the author's memory, conversations, and other communications. This memoir does not reflect all events, characters, and incidents. By sharing the details of her life, the author is not endorsing or recommending any behaviors, lifestyles, or choices that she made. It's the author's hope that each reader will learn something valuable from her story that will help them make positive choices in their own lives.

# Dedication

This book is dedicated to my wonderful partner
and our amazing daughter.

And to my Amish family for keeping me grounded during the storm
when the raging river threatened to carry me away.

# PROLOGUE

A man approached me, his slicked-back hair and goatee flecked with silver, in an expensive-looking suit, and wearing an expression that identified him as someone in charge. He introduced himself as Donovan, the club manager. His eyes scanned my body. "Your friend said you need a job."

Blushing, I looked at Tina, who just stood there with a sly smile on her face. "Oh," I stammered, "I don't think I could ever do that."

"Why not?" Donovan asked.

His eyes studied me, never breaking eye contact, even when I looked away. "I'm too shy."

"Come back to my office," he said. "I want to talk to you some more." He walked away, confident I'd follow, and I did, thinking I had nothing to lose.

Donovan sat behind the desk and motioned for me to sit facing him, then asked me where I was from and my age. Heat spread from my cheeks to my neck and fluttered into my chest as I answered his questions, assuring him I wasn't ready to take my clothes off in front of a bunch of strangers.

"You're young and beautiful," he said. "If you change your mind, you'll make a lot of money. All you need is some confidence. Guys like the shy, innocent look."

"I'm sorry," I said.

He shrugged and motioned toward the door, signaling that I could leave. "If you change your mind, let me know. We'd love to have you."

When I returned to sit with Tina at the bar, we were quickly surrounded by three dancers who introduced themselves as Taylor, Ashley, and Mercedes. They hovered around me, and Mercedes casually asked how I was doing.

"Fine," I replied. The dancers gave me a skeptical look. "I'm a little nervous," I added. "I've never been to a place like this."

They looked at each other as if they shared a secret. "It's okay," one of them reassured me, caressing my arm. "We really want to see you dance on stage."

I almost fell out of my chair. "They must be crazy," I thought.

"Why me?" I asked.

Without answering, they playfully grabbed my arms and pulled me to the dressing room with Tina close behind. One dancer pulled my shirt over my head while another slipped off my skirt. Tina held up two skimpy outfits and they all agreed on a hot pink bikini top with matching booty shorts. I stood in front of the mirror, staring at the pink cloth barely covering my body. Tina had a big smile on her face. "Come on, my friend, you'll be fine. It's fun; just try it." The next song came on, and I heard someone say, "Good luck!" Then they pushed me out the door toward the stage.

"Pour Some Sugar on Me" by Def Leppard burst through the speakers. "I'm not ready for this," I said weakly, but I took the last step onto the stage, and there was no turning back.

"Here I am," I thought. "I might as well make the most of it!" I walked to the pole, grabbed hold of it, and started shaking my hips to the music. Tears welled up in my eyes, but I blinked them away, determined not to let anyone see the terror I felt. I shook my long blond hair so it fell in front of my face, shielding me from the audience. Bending over, I swayed my hips back and forth as I'd seen the other dancers do, trying to look sexy. People clapped and threw money onto the stage. Feeling encouraged, I tilted my head and bit my lower lip as I shyly removed

2

the bikini top and shorts. A wave of hot energy rushed through my entire body. What had I just done? My breasts were exposed for all to see. Everyone, both men and women, flocked to the edge of the stage, and I felt like a rock star.

As the second song began: Def Leppard's "Love Bites," I hooked one finger beneath my panty strap and slowly tugged while bending over until the panties were lying on the floor. I stepped out of them, now completely naked and vulnerable. A moment of panic shot through me as I wondered what my Amish family would think if they could see me now, and I took a moment to pray they'd never find out. When I stepped on stage, I had crossed through a doorway from which I could never return. It felt like only yesterday that I'd worn the long, heavy dresses, aprons, and head coverings that the Amish said would prevent me from burning for eternity. It was a sin to tempt others, explore our own bodies, or acknowledge our sexuality. Everything I'd been taught promised that after tonight I was going straight to hell.

I smiled at the cheering audience, trying to block out my emotions. I remembered Tina's seductive whisper in my ear before I went on stage: "Pretend you're having sex." I got down on my hands and knees, arched my back, and imagined Aaron making love to me, doggy style. But then I replaced his face with the man closest to the stage and pictured the tall, dark stranger taking me right there on stage with the world watching. My fantasy of a normal life with Aaron filled with bowling and matching bathroom sets was over. Instead, here I was in a strip club, crawling around like a cat in heat. Hiding my face behind my hair, I rolled onto my back and spread my legs. People screamed and cheered when I did that. I opened my eyes and it hit me that I was completely naked. I couldn't believe what I was seeing: my own vagina.

# CHAPTER ONE

I was born in Michigan on a farm by a babbling river that my mom and dad warned could carry me away forever if I got too close. Our house was set back from the main road, and on a quiet evening, it was easy to imagine that our home was the only place in the world and that the world ended where the river disappeared into the hills. As a child, I was drawn to the river and its tumbling edges. Despite the jagged boulders, twisted tree roots, and endless eddies in its path, the water tenaciously escaped the boundaries of its bed. The river found a way out no matter what tried to block its way. It was wild and free.

And dangerous, according to my mom and dad, who'd grab me from behind if I approached the edge and snatch me back to safety. We rarely left our secluded little world, and we didn't need to.

For me, an Amish girl, safety meant never watching television, listening to the radio, talking on a phone, or driving a car. Music was forbidden, except for singing in church without accompanying instruments. Books were banned in the name of protection, except for the bible and those approved by the bishops. School ended after the eighth grade, and we went to work on the farm. We were expected to toe the line of the tidy riverbeds drawn for us by the church without question.

One summer, there was a huge rainstorm. I remember watching

from the kitchen window as the sky opened up and spilled over the farm in watery sheets. Dad stood behind me, smoking his pipe. Mom busied herself with shutting the windows and fretting over my younger siblings. Dad pointed to the sky, where bolts of lightning rumbled through the clouds. But I looked at the river, leaping over the boundaries of its narrow bed and tearing through the terrain designed to keep it leashed between the trees. Like a wild animal, it thrashed and resisted what was trying to keep it caged. As water and debris splashed over into the field and through the woods beyond the farm, it became something else. It ceased to be a river. To me, it looked like a living, breathing creature, finally released from its cage, and charging toward its own freedom and destiny.

How I longed to be that river.

Eventually, I'd discover that the river led to another world, very different from our own. This world was called the English, and like the river in a rainstorm, it was wild and free.

It was also forbidden.

I watched from behind our heavy blue curtains as the rainstorm drenched the farm and caused the river to overflow. Mom suddenly yelled out for us to gather the stray chickens into the hen house. We could see at least three of them, shuffling through the grass, confused by the chaos around them. My brothers and I ran into the field after the wayward chickens. We got two of them safely inside, but when we returned, a third chicken had wandered close to the river's edge. The normally neat walls that kept the river in place had been erased by the frothing, raging water breaking free. I watched as the chicken took one last misstep and instantly got swept away, still perched in a watery crest as it rounded a bend, then was gone forever.

I had no idea that one day I would be that chicken in a rain-swept river, one more wild and dangerous than any of us could ever imagine. And my parents were right about the dangers of the river's path but not about what lay at the end.

In one of my earliest memories of meeting the English, I was almost three years old and suffering from bronchitis. Unable to treat me at home, my parents took me to an English doctor. His office was too far to go by horse and buggy, so our English neighbor drove us in a yellow Volkswagen Beetle. I cried because I didn't like the loud noises it made and how fast it went.

Inside the English clinic, a doctor laid me on a metal table covered in paper and put a cold stethoscope on my chest. All the while, I cried, having no idea what was happening to me or why. When the doctor was done, he handed me back to my mom, and we went home in the English neighbor's loud car.

From then on, I was always relieved whenever we returned home, where the noise and chaos of the English world gave way to the simplicity of our Godly ways. I learned to be wary of the English world; like the river, if I got too close, it might carry me away forever.

As members of the Amish community, we were taught to be wary of the outside world and its sinful people. As Swartzentruber Amish, we adhered to the strictest rules of the Amish Order. We had no indoor plumbing; we used an outhouse instead. We shunned most electricity, making use of a small Honda engine to power our washing machine, pump water from the well, and run the table saw. A big diesel engine generated the sawmill. We traveled by horse and buggy, only riding in cars driven by the English when there was an emergency, or we needed to travel farther than a buggy could take us.

Amish children wore aprons that matched long red, green, blue, purple, gray, brown, or black dresses. Our dresses reached the tops of our black shoes and covered our ankles, and black *kapps* (Amish caps) always covered our braided hair. In the summer, we went barefoot. When I turned ten, I continued to wear the long dark dresses, but added dark capes and shorter aprons, called *halsduch* and *schatz* in Pennsylvania Dutch. This was the only language we spoke at home. I wouldn't learn to speak English until I started school.

The Swartzentruber church insisted our way was the only path to Heaven. While I envied the luxuries of the English world, I also felt safe and righteous within the confines of our simple ways. Every day was predictable. On Mondays, we baked cookies and did laundry. We made butter in the churn and grew and canned all our vegetables. On Saturdays, our busiest day, we baked pies, bread, cake, and pudding to last through the week. We also cleaned the house while the men hauled manure from the horse stalls to the fields and tidied up the barn and sheds. I always thought the men's Saturday seemed a lot more fun, even though they were hauling smelly manure out of the barn.

Three times a day, I carefully set the table so the family could sit down and eat together. I was the fourth born and the third girl. Eventually, there would be twelve of us, so my memories are filled with brothers and sisters of various ages. These family meals are some of my favorite memories of being Amish and what I miss most.

Despite the time we spent together as a family, my parents remained a mystery. Any talk of feelings or emotions was frowned upon, as were physical displays of affection. They expected us to show our love for them through unquestioning obedience, and they nodded in approval to express their love for us. Mealtime consisted of us laughing, joking around, and discussing the tasks we completed and others that needed to get done. We often sang German songs as we worked. My parents filled their roles as Mom and Dad, but I never really knew them. My dad, especially, was physically there, yet always just out of reach. He came and went, but I could rarely get his attention, and so he never knew me, either. Most of his time was spent working in the fields, and I often wished I was a boy so I could work alongside him. All week, I looked forward to Saturday night when, after my bath, I got to sit with my dad at his desk with the lid propped open as he sorted the mail and bills from the previous week, then set up to shave. I loved watching as he brought a big mug of warm water from the kitchen, then rinsed his old-fashioned razor and fluffy brush. He'd put a dab of shaving cream on the tip of my nose before spreading it on his face. It made me laugh and feel special, and I craved this attention. It was in those little moments that I felt most loved and protected.

I started to covet the English ways when I met our neighbors across the street, two little girls around our age named Hazel and Autumn. They were as fascinated by us as we were with them. I longed to play at their house, but we weren't allowed, so they came to our house to play hide and seek. Most of all, I wanted to ride their horses, but that was also forbidden. I stayed behind the fence as they walked their horses across the road so I could pet their long, smooth noses.

"Why can't I?" I asked, looking out the window at Hazel and Autumn in their colorful shorts and t-shirts, casually straddling the horses and free to go wherever they pleased.

"Amish girls don't ride horses," Mom said, yanking the curtain shut. "It's against the *Ordnung* (Amish rules)."

"But why?"

Dad gave me a stern look, a reminder that I wasn't supposed to ask so many questions, but Mom replied patiently, "It isn't our way."

They left me at the window to pout, and I lifted the curtain just enough to peek out again. Hazel and Autumn had given up waiting for me and turned back toward the fields. I yearned to run outside and ride with my English friends. I envied their pants and bright colors. Hazel and Autumn could run, jump, and climb without the bloomers, long, dark dresses, and aprons I had to wear. They got to play while we did chores. They got to ride on a school bus, and we had to walk to school. They cuddled store-bought dolls that looked like real babies and smiled back at them compared to our homemade cloth dolls without faces. I wanted to do all the things they could do. Their lives seemed so easy. But while I was jealous, deep down I still felt that their lifestyle was sinful and that God wouldn't like me if I didn't obey my parents.

I felt that our Amish traditions must be keeping me safe and would someday serve me well in a dangerous world. My parents demonstrated their ability to keep me safe through their steadfast and practical choices. They never doubted that their decisions and beliefs were the right ones. While they instilled in us a deep fear of the English world, no matter what, they were calm, stoic, and brave in the face of danger.

One day, I was playing hide and seek with my English neighbors in our yard and almost stepped on a snake. I screamed, terrified, as I realized everyone else had run to safety. I started to cry, wondering why no one bothered to warn me. As I ran around the corner, I saw my mom standing with my playmates. With a shovel in her hand, she calmly said not to worry. She was going to take care of it. We all followed behind, stopping when she warned us to stay back and watched closely as she slowly walked over and killed the snake with the shovel. I felt bad for the snake, but safe and protected by my mom. She was my hero that day. I saw her as a courageous and wise woman. She solved problems while staying calm and instilled confidence in me that I might be brave like her someday.

I started first grade at age six in a one-room schoolhouse. There was one teacher for all classes, first through eighth grade, and my first grade teacher was an Amish teenager named Susan. The only requirement to be an Amish teacher was to be at least fifteen years of age, have completed eighth grade, and be unmarried. When I began, I only knew Pennsylvania Dutch, the language we spoke at home. At school, I learned to read, write, spell, and speak English. At first, learning English filled me with shame. I thought this new language sounded terrible, and I had a hard time pronouncing "th" sounds. During class, if we pronounced a word wrong, the teacher hit us with a yardstick and made us repeat it. In fifth grade, we learned to read, write, and spell in German, which I was already familiar with because Amish bibles and prayer books are all written in German.

Overall, I enjoyed school because it meant I got to be with friends and didn't have to work at home. When it was warm outside, we played softball, kick the can, red rover, hide and seek, gray wolf, and dodgeball. In the winter, when there was snow, we played fox and geese, built snow forts, and went sledding down the big hills surrounding our schoolhouse. Sledding was my favorite. We brought toboggans and heavy-duty plastic bags to school and used them to slide down the icy slopes.

Some of the kids at school didn't like my siblings and me. They refused to play with us and huddled together, whispering, laughing, and pointing at us. They called me a duckling, making fun of my tiny frame and big feet, my big lips and eyes. I became very self-conscious. When we told our parents about how the other kids treated us, they reminded us to treat them with respect.

"Just because other people are mean does not imply that you need to be mean," Mom said.

"Don't fight fire with fire," Dad added.

I only got to go to town once a year in the summer when school was out. And the adventure wasn't guaranteed because the siblings had to take turns. It felt like forever until it was finally my turn. Then I had to wear shoes, which was an odd feeling in the summer. I didn't understand why the English wouldn't let us into their stores without them. Mom and Dad took turns taking us and always gave us a choice to get an ice cream cone or soda. Most of the time, I chose an ice cream cone because I didn't like carbonated soda, and I still don't.

I loved the smell of the market as the magic doors opened automatically. I wanted to touch everything, know what it was for, and how it all worked. But we weren't allowed to touch the English items. Sometimes the English people stared at us, especially the children. We looked so different from them. I wanted to stare back at their bright clothing, jeans, and sneakers. I longed to have the free-flowing hair of the English girls and wear sandals in the summer. I wanted to try glitter nail polish and bring home a Barbie doll. But while the modern world bustled around us, we clip-clopped slowly behind in a horse and buggy, assigned to a way of life that the rest of the world had left long ago.

By the time I was twelve years old, thirteen of us were living in our three-bedroom house. My parents bought a 240-acre farm property across the street. The only building on it was an uninhabitable old brown house. Amish relatives from Minnesota, Iowa, Kentucky, Ohio, and Indiana came to help raise our new home, barns, machinery shed, sawmill, and maple syrup shack. While the men built the barn, the women cooked lunch. My sisters and I, and any other unmarried girls, made lemonade and served the men. Once our barn was complete, we moved all the animals to our new farm. It was a busy and exciting time.

Life on the farm was fun. We had pigs, chickens, rabbits, fourteen horses, and over twenty cows. Instead of tractors, the horses plowed the fields and pulled the wagons. Each year, we planted ten to fifteen acres of corn in the spring, and in the fall, we husked and picked each ear by hand. My parents sometimes kept us kids home from school to help husk, and we all worked as a family. We also grew hay, spelt, and oats. I loved helping my dad and brothers put up the hay in the barn. I worked in the fields every chance I got alongside my brothers. It felt so free and peaceful.

Even though mom had twelve children, she never talked about being pregnant or where my new baby brothers and sisters came from. Every couple of years, we asked mom and dad where the new baby came from, and they responded that it was God's way of blessing us. I didn't understand how or why God would decide to bring us another baby. This was confusing. But I started putting two and two together when I noticed her belly had grown, and then there was a baby, and her belly would get smaller again. Eventually, I figured out that my mom was the baby maker. Even so, I still wasn't sure how she was making the babies or why they were in her belly.

Before I turned thirteen, my mom pulled me aside. She told me I would soon get my "cluck" and that I would have to wear shoes everywhere I went for the whole week I was afflicted, even in the summer. I couldn't do any heavy lifting or gardening.

My cluck turned out to be my period. Mom never explained what was happening to me, but she showed me how to rip up towels for pads, secure them with bobby pins, then wash and reuse them. My brothers had no clue, so they made fun of us for wearing our shoes in the summer and taking breaks from chores.

My fascination with the English world grew when I met my new English neighbor, Julia. She was a few years younger than me and came over to play and help out on the farm. My parents weren't pleased with her English ways, but they tolerated her. Julia had so much fun riding in the horse-drawn buggy. She thought it was the greatest thing ever. I thought the same about her bicycle. I wanted to ride it, but the *Ordnung* said I couldn't. I wondered why we had so many unfair rules. What was so bad about a bicycle?

When I went to the neighbors' houses to bring baked goods or vegetables, I lingered to peer at their TV or listen to the radio. I couldn't help it. I just hoped I wouldn't go to hell because of my wandering eyes and ears. I felt guilty for wanting these things because the *Ordnung* forbade them. I especially fantasized about having a phone. I thought it would be cool to just pick up the phone and talk to my friends anytime I wanted to.

That year on Christmas Day, my brothers and I went to our cousins' house to go ice skating while their parents were away on vacation. When we arrived, the curtains were drawn, which was unusual for the time of day. I followed the Amish tradition of walking through the unlocked door, unannounced as my brothers unhitched the horse.

As soon as my cousin, Sam, saw me, he grabbed a radio off the table, shoved it under his jacket, and ran into his parents' bedroom. The rest of my cousins were just as shocked to see me as I was to see their radio, but when Sam returned from the bedroom without any radio, they all acted like nothing happened. The afternoon was awkward, and we never went ice skating. I could tell they were worried that I was going to tattle. My brothers had no idea that I'd discovered my cousins' radio. They asked our cousins to go ice skating, but the cousins said they didn't feel like it.

I was so confused and angry. I even snuck into their parents' bedroom and searched, but I didn't find the radio. For a moment, I doubted what I'd seen. Although I'd fantasized about having a radio, I never planned on living out my fantasies and getting one. I wondered how my cousins could be so disrespectful of our traditions, and I couldn't wait to get home and tell my parents. My Uncle Henry was working for us at the time, so I found him in the cow barn and told him first. He asked if I was sure I saw a radio. When I insisted that I was sure, he told me to sit on a hay bale and listen.

"Some of the Amish kids have radios," he explained. "It's okay if you don't tattle and tell your parents."

I couldn't believe what my Uncle Henry was saying. He laughed. "Promise me you won't tattle, and I promise not to tattle when you get your first radio," he said.

My anger turned to joy when I realized that maybe one day, I could also have a radio. I promised Uncle Henry that I wouldn't tattle on my cousins. Two weeks later, my cousin brought over a radio and introduced me to country music. Suddenly, music was all I could think about, and I wondered how I ever lived without it. I especially loved listening to Joe Diffie's song, "Pickup Man," and pretending I was English. When John Michael Montgomery sang "Sold," I fantasized that I was the English girl in the song, and pictured myself dressed in jeans, a t-shirt, cowboy boots, and a cowgirl hat.

At that moment, I realized I was missing out on many harmless activities because I was Amish. I stopped believing in the Amish lifestyle and rules. I wanted to be English and experience everything life had to offer. I was ready to ride the river around the bend into the great unknown. I wasn't old enough yet to leave and be on my own, but I decided it was okay to keep secrets from my parents.


The summer after eighth grade, I turned fourteen, and like most Amish children, my formal education ended. Girls were expected to work as *mauds* (maids) for other Amish families in exchange for room and board, and a small stipend paid to their parents. My parents sent me to my Aunt Elizabeth and Uncle Abraham to help on their farm, in their garden, and take care of their kids. This also served as formal training to ensure I became a good Amish housewife and mother.

I looked forward to being a *maud*. I'd still be doing chores all day, but I wouldn't be stuck at home. Going to a new place with new responsibilities made me feel grown up and free.

Eventually, though, the excitement of the new faces and routines wore off and I found the daily chores tedious again. As my English neighbors went off to the local high school, I became increasingly envious. I fantasized about running away to be free to ride horses and bicycles.

I bought myself a little radio with headphones, which I hid under my mattress. Before I went to sleep, I slipped on the headphones and listened to country music beneath the covers.

During my first season as a *maud*, I went home every other weekend. While at home, my sisters and I kept the radio hidden in the barn or attic. We had to be careful that our younger siblings didn't hear the music and tell our parents. If my dad found out, he'd make us smash the radio with a sledgehammer. At least that's what other Amish dads did when they found their kids' radios. But we never got caught. One by one, we told our younger siblings. Thankfully, they never tattled. They loved music as much as I did. My younger sisters slipped a few times by singing country music songs in front of my mom. Suspicious, she asked where they heard such songs. I quickly said they must have heard it from vehicles driving past on the road. We could tell she was skeptical, but she accepted our answer.

The summer I turned fifteen felt especially hot, and the chore of pulling on huge, heavy bloomers that made me sweat beneath my dress became unbearable. I hated my homemade underwear, which looked more like shorts. Even without the underdress I wore in the winter, my *graddle* felt like an oven. That's what we called our "privates" in Pennsylvania Dutch. On a muggy Sunday morning, standing in the bedroom I shared with my sisters, Emma and Rachel, I yanked off my bloomers and crumpled them into a ball.

"I can't wear these today," I declared, swishing my bare pelvis around in the fabric of the long dress, hiding my secret. Even with the heavy layers covering everything, I felt free.

"What are you going to wear then?" Emma asked.

"Nothing!" I replied. "It's too hot. Who's going to know if you don't tell?" I gave them a stern look, silently reminding them that I also knew their secrets, and handed my discarded bloomers to Emma.

"Why are you handing them to me?" Emma asked.

"Either get rid of them or join me," I challenged her.

"You're on your own," Emma declared.

"Fine," I said, burying my bloomers in the back of the dresser.

They just shook their heads with disapproval. Then we got into the buggy and headed to church.

I loved the feeling of being naked underneath my dress. When I stepped outside, a breeze fluttered between my thighs and through my bare *graddle*. Walking into the church behind my sisters, I realized that when the sun hit the backs of their dresses, I could see the outline of their bloomers, and became painfully aware that anyone behind me would see I had none. Shielding the back of my dress with my hands, I let my mom pass so I could walk behind her. Even though I worried about getting caught, I also felt very naughty, which excited me.

Once I got away with not wearing bloomers, I started looking for English clothes at yard sales. I tried to be inconspicuous as I rummaged through the boxes of bright t-shirts and blue jeans, holding them up against my body and soliciting my sisters' opinions. One box offered a few open packages of striped English "bikini-style" panties with elastic trim. For only 25 cents, I was tempted to buy them.

Rachel wrinkled her nose. "You don't know where they've been." I reluctantly put them back. "Don't worry, Naomi," she assured me. "We'll go to the English store this weekend, and you can buy all the sexy English panties you want."

I bought the jeans, some t-shirts, and a pair of white shorts that had a rip on the backside. The yard sale proprietor said it was supposed to be there, and she called it a peek-a-boo.

"Drives the boys crazy." She giggled as she tucked them into a bag along with the other clothing. "Have fun!"

Now that we were out of school, Mom and Dad sometimes let my sisters and I go to town without them. The next time we went, I headed straight to the back of the Dollar Store to find the English panties. Underwear of all colors, shapes, and sizes hung individually on tiny plastic hangers on racks. Others came in packs of three or more wrapped in plastic. Never had I imagined there could be so many styles and colors. I let my fingers slide over a pink lace pair that looked to be missing its backside. Three thin strips of lace were all that held a triangle of fabric together.

"What does this do?" I asked the sales clerk.

She burst out laughing but then composed herself and said, "That's called a thong."

"A thong?"

Both my sisters turned red. I picked out a variety of styles and colors: pink lace, red satin, and a thong made of black fishnet material. I felt shy and awkward when it was time to pay, and I hoped no one was looking at me or the panties I was buying.

Back in our room at home, we giggled and shushed each other as I tried them on. The slippery material slid up and down my backside and felt funny, but I loved the secret feeling of wearing them. Amish underwear was treated like a dirty secret among the Amish. When we did laundry, we hung them on the inside lines with bigger clothes, such as sheets or long dresses, on the outside lines to shield them from passersby. We didn't want my brothers and dad to see them either. Our brothers picked on us when they spied underwear hanging on the line. They'd laugh and say someone forgot to hide the bloomers, so the English probably all saw them as they drove by. The thought that the English might have seen my bloomers made me uncomfortable.

Yet I was so thrilled with my new English panties that I started wearing them to church. My friends and I giggled in the outhouse about them after services. Amish families took turns hosting church services in their homes, so the only private place was the outhouse. I took tremendous joy in being the instigator. I directed the participating parties to the outhouse, and we locked the door behind us so the other girls couldn't come in. We whispered and giggled as they admired and touched my English panties while taking turns sitting on the plywood with a hole carved out to pee. Other girls knocked on the door, urging us to hurry up. When we finally opened the door, they glared at us, and one girl angrily asked what was so funny.

"Sorry," we said through peals of laughter and brushed past them.

I wasn't a fan of hosting church services because we had to clean the whole house, including the walls and the yard. The Swartzentruber Amish only go to church every other Sunday, so it wasn't something we did often, but it was a major production when we did. We removed most of the furniture and set up several rows of wooden benches in the kitchen and living room. The married men and boys sat on one side and the *Mummies,* the oldest women, sat with the older girls on the other side. Married women with children and younger girls sat in the kitchen.

After services, we served a big home-cooked meal. We weren't allowed to do any other work on Sundays except essential chores like taking care of the animals. We were also forbidden to buy anything or even water the garden. Sunday was considered a holy day of church or rest. I loved the Sundays we didn't have to go to church because I got to sleep in. As much as I dreaded the preparation and rules surrounding church, I loved listening to the congregation singing in German. Without any music, their voices sounded beautiful and otherworldly. Before I became rebellious, I looked forward to church and visiting with my cousins and friends. After I became a teenager, I couldn't have cared less. I napped during the sermons.

I started sneaking across the woods to visit our English neighbors, Jared and Kimberly, where I broke more rules. They let me swim in their pool and watch movies. At first, I had no idea movies were fictional or that the people in them were actors. I thought they were real, like documentaries. Early on, we watched a scary movie, and I went home thinking I'd witnessed all those people die. I had horrible nightmares. I loved the pool though. I'd never been in a large body of water before. My heavy Amish dress weighed me down, so I just paddled around, but it felt good to get into the water on a hot summer day.

That Fall, an English neighbor brought us a camera. It was a secret that we couldn't tell our parents because, like radios, cameras were forbidden. We took pictures of each other when our parents weren't around. I let my hair down, feeling sexy, happy, and free. The jeans, T-shirts, and panties I bought were hidden in the attic, along with the camera. I wore them on Sundays when my parents were away and our Amish friends came over to visit. At first, I felt self-conscious showing the curves of my body, but I quickly grew comfortable and enjoyed the thrill of wearing English clothes. I also painted my fingernails red. I felt so English, and that made me feel pretty. Doing whatever I wanted was a little taste of freedom.

One day, my cousins and I walked to the neighbors' house to call our English friends, Bob and Bobby, to come pick us up. Bob and Bobby bought us beer and cigarettes, then took us to their house in town where we drank, smoked, and watched music videos. That was the first time I saw sexy dancing. The people in the music videos looked so happy, and I wondered how they had the courage to sing and dance in front of the world.

I ended up drinking way too much. When Bob and Bobby dropped us off, I was so sick that I didn't know what was going on, nor did I care. My cousins helped me take the polish off my nails and made sure my hair was pinned up. Thank goodness Mom and Dad had company and didn't come to oversee the cow-milking. I tried to help my sisters, but I was drunk and throwing up. I slept in the hay until the chores were done.

Every summer, we had parties where we picked berries and made homemade ice cream, and then put the freshly picked berries on top. At one of these parties, all of us older girls snuck across the street to hang out with the English neighbor boys we had crushes on. We sat in their yard and talked and laughed. I thought they were so cool in their shorts and tank tops. Their smooth, bare arms and hairy legs turned me on. I had fantasies about sneaking out and going for rides in their trucks.

Of course, we were forbidden to have sexual relations with any boy, especially the English. I felt shy, but that didn't stop me from talking and flirting with them. Suddenly, we heard people yelling our names. It was getting dark and time to go home. We ran back across the road, where everyone seemed confused by our absence. They'd been looking for us.

We quickly defused the situation by telling them we were hanging out in the field behind the shed. The elders seemed concerned, but no one said anything to us about it after that night.

The following Sunday at church, my cousins, Ivy and Ada, told me and our other cousin, Ella, about the new English guys, Mason and Myles, they'd been hanging out with. We stood outside just after the service, far enough to be seen but not heard.

"We snuck out last night," Ada whispered. Ivy blushed and looked away, confirming there was more to come.

"What did you do?" Ella crept closer, waiting for the answer.

"We had sex with them," Ada smiled, clearly enjoying the shock on our faces. Ella gasped.

"What was it like?" I asked.

Ivy broke her silence by giggling.

"What's so funny?" I asked.

Ada playfully draped an arm around each of our shoulders. "Why should I tell you when you can find out for yourselves?"

Ella grabbed her arm. "What do you mean, find out for ourselves?"

Ada handed me a piece of paper. "Here's their phone number so you can call them."

My parents went on vacation a few weeks later, and Ella and I decided it was time to sneak out. We stopped at a neighbor's house to use their phone. Neither of us wanted to make the call because we'd never met these boys, but finally, I decided I would do it since I was the thrill seeker. Shaking, I picked up the phone and dialed their number to ask if they could pick us up on Saturday night at ten o'clock. They said yes.

As Saturday approached, I was nervous, secretly wondering what sex for the first time would feel like. Would I like it and crave more? What if my parents found out? Why were we doing this? Was it the rush of sneaking out and doing something new? We promised to look out for each other no matter what.

# CHAPTER TWO

Saturday night finally came. Ella came over; we let our hair down and put on our English panties and fancy Sunday underdresses. Mason and Myles showed up in a little Chevy truck. My cousin sat in the middle, I sat on Myles's lap, and they offered us a beer. Everything was so awkward at first because we didn't know each other.

"What do you want to do?" Mason asked. His eyes shifted nervously to Myles as he tried to hide a smile.

Ella shrugged, so the boys looked at me. "We don't care," I answered for both of us. "We just wanted to get out of the house."

We drove around the country roads, drank beer, and shared a cigarette until they found a field with a long driveway and Mason parked the truck. Myles asked me if I wanted to get out with him, so I did.

At that moment, I knew we were going to have sex. I was excited and nervous. I'd never had sex before and didn't know what to do, so I shyly followed his lead. Myles took off his pants and laid them on the snow-covered field, then told me to lay on my back on top of his pants. I did, then lifted my underdress and slid my new sexy panties down to my ankles. Myles put on a condom. I shivered, worried it might hurt, as the cold air hit my bare legs. Then I remembered Ivy's giggling and Ada's smile. I relaxed. He got on top of me and I felt him fill me up. The secret space between my legs popped and swelled open to receive him.

He thrust gently at first, then harder and harder, breathing more heavily. I just lay there, not knowing what to do. But five or six thrusts and that was it. Fast, easy, and painless. I wondered what the big deal was. Ella was inside the truck having sex with Mason. It was her first time, too. It was all so thrilling, but I was glad he didn't last long because it was so cold and snowy.

When I saw Ella again a few days later, she was scared. We were both bleeding a bit and didn't know why.

"If I'm bleeding, does that mean I'm pregnant?" Ella asked.

"Didn't he use a condom?" I whispered the last word, even though we were alone.

"Yes, I watched him put it on."

"Then you have nothing to worry about," I assured her.

Thankfully, we didn't get pregnant. I felt exhilarated. I knew it was the most taboo thing I could do and couldn't wait to do it again.

We continued to sneak out and meet up at least one Sunday a month to have sex with Myles and Mason. Usually, sneaking out was my idea. I waited until after everyone went to bed, then left the front door unlocked to get back inside the house unnoticed. Many Sunday afternoons, the boys picked up my cousins and me and took us to their home to watch country music videos and porn. Watching porn was almost as much fun for me as having sex. I loved learning how to have sex, then doing it with Myles, Mason, and their friends. I loved having sex with different guys that I barely knew. I didn't have orgasms, but I got pleasure because I enjoyed feeling so rebellious.

One Saturday, I made an extra cherry pie to take to the English boys when I snuck out the next day. It took careful planning because I had to ensure mom overlooked the extra pie. The following evening after dinner, I opened the pantry window and placed the extra pie on a big pail beneath the window. Rachel and I went downstairs as if we were going to the outhouse, then I sent her back as a decoy. I ran up the road with the pie to meet the boys. Suddenly, I heard my parents shouting my name in distress, and I threw the pie into a ditch. My parents were upset. They didn't believe I was out jogging and thought I was running away.

Mason and Myles were waiting for me at the crossroads. I felt so bad that I couldn't call and tell them what happened. I worried they might not come to pick me up again because I'd wasted their time.

The next evening, my brother told me he saw a pie in the ditch as he drove by in the buggy. Oh no! I was busted if my parents saw the pie in the ditch. After dark, I ran up the road to hide the pie. The ants were already eating it; they attacked my hand as I buried it in the grass. Later in the week, I looked for the pie, but all that was left was the empty aluminum pan, a reminder of how I nearly got caught.

I didn't want to sneak out to have fun anymore. I couldn't handle the Amish rules. I wanted to do what I wanted, when I wanted, and with whomever I wanted, without feeling bad about it. I knew for sure I was going to run away.

I began to resent my father for blindly following the Amish *Ordnung*. I didn't want to be in the same room with him alone for fear he would lecture me about my rebellious behavior. I thought he and his ridiculous rules were horrible, and I didn't want any part of him or them.

"Naomi, cover your hair!" Mom stopped me as we walked into a neighbor's house for church. I sighed, tucking my long blond strands back underneath. "And pull up your cape!" she added. I tugged at my collar. Mom's eyes questioned me as if she knew I wanted to show off, which I did. The Amish rules say that the woman's cape can't slide below her shoulders, and her *kapp* must cover her hair. But I felt deliciously naughty when I didn't look like everyone else. Once she was satisfied, Mom continued into church, and I dutifully followed. As soon as we separated, I loosened my hair and cape again.

Whenever my parents went on vacation, we invited our Amish friends over to listen to the radio and drink beer. We let our hair down, played cards, and took pictures. We had so much fun, and it was a little taste of freedom.

At sixteen-and-a-half years old, the church required that I join "The

Singing," a social gathering for Amish teens in the evenings after church. The Singing was supposed to allow Amish teens to socialize without sin while scoping out potential mates. But many of them were my cousins; we often just drank beer and smoked cigarettes. Even so, I never felt like I belonged.

Afterward, the boys could take the girls on a "date." On a traditional Amish date, the boy escorts a girl to her home, past her parents, and into the girl's bed. They are expected to spend the night together without having sex, which is considered perfectly normal by Amish parents.

Shortly after I joined, two Amish boys from the south district came to our house to ask for dates. When we heard them come up the stairs, Emma and Rachel ran into their room, and I hid under my bed covers. The boys stopped across the hall to ask my sisters where I was. Thankfully, they said they didn't know. I heard them walk into my room. I held my breath under the covers, praying they wouldn't discover me. I lay there, frozen, as they checked under the bed and opened the dresser drawers.

When we heard them walk down the hall to my brother's room, Emma and I ran and hid in a ditch outside until they left. I didn't want to date the Amish boys, but they were persistent. Six of them grabbed me one night after The Singing as I walked back to my buggy.

"Who do you want to date?" They each hung onto a piece of my clothing so I couldn't escape.

"No one!" I yelled and slipped from their grasp. I only got a few feet before they caught me again and threw me into the buggy with my second cousin, Daniel.

Daniel said "Git" to the horse and started in the direction of my house. He tried to make small talk on the way to my first so-called Amish date, but I refused to answer. When we got home, my sister said I could borrow her bed. Daniel tried to cuddle and kiss me, which is what we were expected to do, but I refused. I lay flat against the edge of the bed and pretended to sleep, but I stayed wide awake. Finally, just before dawn, Daniel left. I was so relieved.

Now all I could think about was running away—no more silly Amish dates. I wanted the English boys! I had no idea where I would go; I just knew it was time to leave.

One hot July morning, I got a chance to put my plan into action as I picked strawberries in the garden after breakfast. My parents were out of town, my sisters were working in the house, and my brothers were in the fields. Kevin, the English truck driver who delivered logs to our sawmill, stopped to buy a few pints.

Kevin was friendly and quick-witted whenever he stopped by for eggs, baked goods, vegetables, or strawberries. He was balding with a goatee. He wasn't handsome by any stretch of the imagination, but he was flirtatious, and I enjoyed talking to him. I always found an excuse to talk to any English people passing by. That morning, I had an epiphany that Kevin might help me. I was getting desperate and knew it was risky, but I couldn't think of anyone else to ask. I wanted to be English so badly that it was a risk I was willing to take. I decided to make my move. "It's time to escape Amishland," I said. "Can I stay with you for a while?"

Kevin looked surprised. "Are you crazy?"

"I might be crazy, but I'm serious," I said.

Kevin said he didn't know; he'd think about it and let me know. I made him promise not to tell anyone.

A week later, he returned and said I could live with his mom if I helped take care of her. I wanted to scream with joy, but I restrained my excitement. Kevin ran his eyes over my body. Even though my long dress covered me, my body felt exposed. "You're a grown woman now," he said. "I can see those pretty curves wanting to burst out of that dress."

I must have blushed because he smiled and asked me to come to the barn with him. I looked around to make sure no one was watching and nervously followed him into an empty horse stall. He unzipped his pants and asked me to get on my knees. I hesitated, knowing what was expected of me. I'd never done anything like this, although I'd seen it done in the porn videos I watched with the English boys. I wasn't sure I could do it, but he persisted. So, I went for it and gave him a blowjob right there in the empty horse stall. He put his hands on the back of my head to help guide me. I gagged slightly and thought I might vomit, but he quickly orgasmed in my mouth. I was disgusted by the taste. He told me to swallow like a good girl. My eyes watered, and my heart beat a million miles a minute. What a rush! "I must be insane," I thought. I wondered if I enjoyed it or just liked how naughty I felt afterward. It was my craziest secret yet.

When I returned to the house, my sisters asked what I was doing with Kevin in the barn. I told them he wanted to look at the kittens, but I don't think they believed me. I didn't care. I'd already told Kevin I would call when I was ready to leave. I wondered if I was brave enough. Carrying all my secrets felt like a great burden, and I didn't know how much longer I could live like that.

There were days when I was conflicted about my decision. My sisters knew something was wrong, but I refused to talk to them about it. I was waiting for the right time, but it never seemed to come. I knew I needed to leave before I was eighteen and they forced me to get baptized. Once baptized, I'd be shunned for life if I did something the elders didn't approve of. Only time would tell if I could gather the strength to leave the Amish.

Before I left, I had to find my birth certificate. We were milking cows one night when I told everyone I had to go to the outhouse. Instead, I went inside, stole my birth certificate from my dad's desk, and ran upstairs to hide it in my dresser. I prayed my dad wouldn't notice it was missing the next night while he was shaving and going through the mail. Thankfully he didn't, but I worried as I gathered my belongings and hid them in a grocery bag in the attic. I felt guilty about leaving my family. I knew they would be deeply hurt and concerned about me. However, I also knew I had to think about myself and my future. It was so hard for me to imagine any future other than being Amish. I worried my family wouldn't accept me and I'd always be an outcast. My sisters kept asking if I was okay. I told them I was great. But deep down, I wondered if I could really run away from my family, the very people that loved me so much.

That night after we ate supper and did our chores, Rachel, Emma, and I took strawberries to our English neighbors, Jared and Kimberly. While they were outside visiting, I went into the house and used Jared and Kimberly's phone to call Kevin, but he wasn't home, so I left a message letting him know I wanted to leave at midnight and the location to pick me up.

Everything was normal back home, but I wondered if Kevin had received my message. At nine o'clock, a truck pulled into the driveway, and I looked out the window to see Kevin and a woman in the passenger seat. My heart skipped. I didn't understand why he was so early. The plan was to sneak out while everyone was sleeping. I couldn't get away otherwise. I hoped he hadn't spoiled my plan.

My family went outside to greet them, and my dad asked why they had come by so late. I heard them say they'd come to buy strawberries. I sighed with relief and greeted them as if everything was normal. While everyone crowded around the driver's side, chatting with Kevin, I walked to the other side of the truck. Kevin's passenger rolled down the window and in a soft voice, introduced herself as Christina, Kevin's wife. He'd never mentioned his wife before, but in the moment I didn't care. I just wanted to run away and didn't want them to mess it up.

Whispering, I told Christina to remind Kevin to pick me up at the crossroads, two hundred yards up the road, at midnight. She nodded and replied that they would be there to pick me up. My face felt hot, and I was trembling because I was so afraid of getting caught. Emma and some of my younger siblings trickled over to talk to Christina, and I pretended everything was normal even though I felt nauseous and worried.

They left, and I waited for everyone to go to sleep. For some reason, everyone stayed up later than usual, and it was almost midnight by the time they were all in bed. The floorboards seemed to creak louder than usual as I tiptoed to the attic to get my stuff. When I returned to my room, Emma stood in the doorway.

"Are you running away?"

"No," I insisted. "I can't sleep. I went to get a book."

"I don't believe you," she said. "I saw Kevin and Christina up at the crossroads."

"That could be anyone," I replied. "Other people have trucks like that."

"You are busted," she said.

I was a terrible liar. I looked away. "You're wrong, and you need to go to sleep because it's getting late."

"I can't sleep because our family will be devastated if you leave," she replied.

I went to bed and pretended to sleep, hoping she would get tired. I worried Kevin and Christina would leave if I didn't show up soon, and sure enough, ten minutes later, I heard their truck pull away in the distance. Emma had ruined my plan! I had no idea when I could leave, if not that night. I begged her to go to sleep, but she insisted that she wouldn't let me run away. Finally I stopped replying and, eventually, I heard her go to bed. It was two-thirty in the morning.

I crawled to the hallway, listening to her breathe. It sounded like she was sleeping, so I left a note on my dresser telling my family I didn't want to be Amish anymore, grabbed my belongings, and pushed aside the screen of my bedroom window. I climbed onto the roof, crawled to the edge, and jumped twelve feet to the ground. Then I took off running into the darkness. I could hear the thump of my heart beating as I ran, scared I would hear Emma's voice calling my name.

Kevin and Christina had already left, so I huddled in an old shed up the road, alone in the dark for the rest of the night, trying to figure out my next move. I had no idea what I'd do after getting to Kevin and Christina's. The unknown was so scary. Maybe I wasn't meant to be English. Three hours alone in a dark shed was a long time to think about my future. I didn't know much about Kevin and Christina, but if I went back home, I'd probably never leave again. I didn't realize that running away was so difficult.

As the sun rose, I could see and hear my family in the distance as they started their morning chores. I worried they'd come looking for me and realized I needed to hide somewhere else. I took one last look at the house and ran through the woods behind the farm to use the neighbor's phone to call Kevin and Christina again. The neighbors were still sleeping, so I hid in the woods nearby until their lights turned on, then knocked on the door. My hands shook as I dialed.

The new pickup spot was another half-mile through the woods, and

I ran the whole way, hiding from buggies passing on the road. I was so afraid someone would see me and tell my parents. I listened for the sound of Kevin's loud truck and wondered what was taking so long. Two hours went by before I went to another English house to use the phone. Once again, Christina answered. She said they'd driven back and forth past the meeting spot looking for me, but they were in Christina's car, not Kevin's truck. It felt like forever since I'd jumped off the roof of my house, but Kevin and Christina finally picked me up. When we arrived at their house, I was exhausted and anxious, but I realized I'd escaped. I took a deep breath, and finally began to feel free.

# CHAPTER THREE

Christina suggested I eat something and put out sandwich ingredients, telling me to help myself. Even though I hadn't eaten anything since the night before, I didn't feel hungry. I was shaking. I don't know if it was nerves or my body needing food, but I finally made myself a sandwich. They laughed, and I asked what was so funny.

"Why do you only use one piece of bread for your sandwich?" Kevin asked.

I didn't know what he meant. I looked down at my piece of bread wrapped around the meat and cheese.

"You can use two pieces," Kevin explained.

"Oh, the Amish only use one piece," I said, blushing.

They chuckled, and I realized I had much to learn about the English and their world. I couldn't finish my sandwich because I was anxious. What if my family found me? What would happen to me? What would my life be like as an English girl? I had such mixed feelings. Kevin and Christina assured me that I'd be okay. Christina was a devout Christian with a sweet demeanor, and her hair was dyed blonde and permed. I appreciated Christina's kindness toward me.

She suggested I take a shower. "Have you ever shaved your legs and armpits?" she asked. I shook my head no. I'd never even taken a shower, let alone shaved. Amish girls aren't supposed to shave their legs and armpits. Christina showed me how to turn on the water and shave, and I took a long shower. It felt so good I didn't want to get out. I'd been missing out.

I had sixty dollars with me and thought I was rich! The concept of money and buying things was unfamiliar to me. Christina suggested we go to Walmart to buy clothes and other things I'd need for life in the English world.

I told her how much I had to spend.

Christina waved me away. "That's fine. I'll pay for some things if you don't have enough."

I felt bad, but Christina insisted. She wanted to help me and show me the English ways. As soon as we walked into Walmart, I felt overwhelmed. I'd never seen so many clothes in my life and didn't know where to start. I stood there, frozen. Christina told me to go ahead and try some things on, but I was too scared to touch anything. She held up some blouses and asked if I liked them. I didn't know. I had no idea what size I was or what style I liked. And English clothes cost so much. I picked up a pair of shorts. "Don't be shy," Christina called out.

I'd never worn shorts in public, but I always wanted to and found a pair of black ones that I liked. Christina thought they were too short, but she encouraged me to get them, then picked out some longer shorts, shirts, and a hot pink, one-piece bathing suit for me to try on. I found it odd that I could try on the clothes before buying them. Christina also suggested I get pads for my period.

I politely asked her to get them for me because I was uncomfortable picking them out. Later, she showed me how to put them into my panties. I thanked Christina for her help, humbled by her generosity. She assured me that she was committed to teaching me the ways of the English lifestyle.

I stayed with Kevin and Christina for a few days, then moved in with Kevin's mom, Tammy. When I told her I'd never eaten fast food, Tammy immediately took me to Burger King. I expected she'd park the car and we'd go inside. I'd never heard of a drive-thru and wondered why we parked out back next to pictures of the food. Tammy asked what I wanted to eat, and I said I had no idea. I was still waiting to go inside when I was startled by a voice asking us what we wanted. I gasped. Tammy explained that we give our order to the voice coming from the speaker, then pull up to a window to pick up our food. I thought that was so cool. I didn't know what I wanted and asked Tammy to order something for me. Besides, I was too shy to talk to the voice coming from the speaker. Tammy ordered me a Whopper, which I enjoyed very much.

Tammy lived in an old, cluttered farmhouse on an isolated road. I got bored there by myself with nothing to do. Sometimes I looked through her boxes of clutter to occupy my time and went for walks in the woods. I tried to enjoy the time to myself, but it was so different from life on the farm, where I got up early and worked all day. I felt insufficient and lazy. I even thought about going back to my family. Kevin and Christina didn't have a second bedroom, so I couldn't stay with them. I wanted to get a job, but they said I should take my time to learn the ways of the English world. They would support me financially until I was eighteen, and in return, I cleaned their house and washed their vehicles. But I could only clean and wash so much. Some days I felt like I was going crazy. I missed my family, but I knew if I went back, I might never have the courage to leave again. I chose to be patient and stay English.

When Kevin invited me to a party one night, I jumped at the chance. Finally! My English life was beginning. He made me promise not to tell Christina. I agreed, ready for some excitement. I couldn't wait to get out of the house and do something fun.

We pulled up to a small RV, and Kevin introduced me to his business partner, Jason, and their friend, Myles. He looked familiar, and it turned out he was the same Myles who'd taken my virginity. We gathered around a bonfire and drank beer. I didn't mean to get drunk, but I didn't know how much was too much. I vaguely remember the guys having sex with me one at a time until I threw up.

The sun was coming up when I awoke next to the toilet in Tammy's bathroom. Through my fog, I tried to remember the details of the previous night. It was the first time I ever blacked out from drinking, and unfortunately, it wouldn't be the last. Everything at the party was a blur: I had no memory of Kevin driving me home, and I had a terrible throbbing headache from my hangover. I didn't think I'd have any big secrets once I became English, but I was wrong. That night became one of many secrets I'd try to forget.

The following days and weeks were filled with guilt and shame. I hoped no one would ever find out I had sex with several men in one night. Kevin was thirty-three years old. I was seventeen and thought it was my fault. I had a heavy feeling in my stomach, like a big rock that wouldn't go away. Over time, it seemed to lessen, or so I thought. Perhaps I got used to the rock being there. I thought maybe it was the price of being free. At least I wasn't being confined or controlled by the Amish, but I had no one to talk to about it. And eventually, the rock created a hole that I could never fill.

At the same time, I had strong feelings for Kevin. He gave me the emotional connection that I'd craved so badly but never got from my father. He was the first man to really see me by acknowledging the things that made me unique. To Kevin, I wasn't just cute and pretty and nice to have around. He told me I was smart and capable and even special. He made me feel safe and wanted. I knew it was wrong. Christina was kind and loving and treated me like the daughter she never had. People often asked if she was my mother, and we usually said yes. I felt terrible about lying to her, but I was trapped by my affection for both Christina and Kevin, and powerless to choose one over the other.

My dad kept calling Kevin's house, insisting he return me to my family. Even though I'd left a note, they were convinced I'd been kidnapped. Kevin denied it, and my dad called the police, who threatened to search Kevin's house. Kevin didn't want to get charged with kidnapping, so he finally told the police where I was. Tammy wasn't home, so Kevin told me to sit on her front porch and wait. I was terrified they might take me home or to jail, but Kevin assured me everything would be okay. Even so, I wanted to run and hide. English life wasn't as easy as I thought it would be.

Two police officers walked up to the front porch and asked if I was okay.

I looked down at my hands and realized I was shaking. "I'm just nervous to talk to you," I replied.

One of the officers nodded and wrote something in his notebook. He asked if I was safe, with food to eat and clothes to wear.

He waited until I nodded, then asked to come inside and look around. They opened the refrigerator, and I showed them where I kept my clothes. Finally, they said, "Everything looks good." Before leaving, they made me promise to write a letter to my family and let them know where I was and that I was safe, and I promised I would. They said they'd stop at my family's house to let them know where I was.

I smiled and nodded as I closed the door, relieved, but disappointed they were going to tell my family. That meant my parents could come try and coax me home any time.

And they did. One day, Tammy and I came home to find buggy tracks in the driveway. I knew that meant my parents had come looking for me. I was happy I'd missed them. I don't know what I would have done otherwise. I hoped they wouldn't come back, but that was wishful thinking. They returned, but I was never there when they arrived. I don't think I could have faced my parents. They were shattered, and I'm sure I would've broken down and cried if I'd seen them. I missed them so much, but I didn't want to go back. Being English was all I'd thought about for so long, and I wanted to give it a chance.

The hardest part was being alone. I'd been surrounded by my big family all my life and suddenly found myself alone for days on end. I learned a lot about myself during those days. I cried and prayed. I thought for sure I'd burn in hell for eternity. Tammy, Kevin, and Christina all reassured me that I wouldn't burn in hell because I'd just been brainwashed by the Amish.

One morning, Kevin and I were eating breakfast at the table as we often did. Christina had already left for work, and Kevin had the day off. He looked at me thoughtfully as he chewed, as if carefully considering what to say. Usually, he was quick to say whatever was on his mind. I knew something was up. I raised one eyebrow, something I'd practiced in preparation for being English.

"Have you ever had an orgasm, Naomi?"

I blushed at his sudden question. "No, I don't know how." I looked out the window. "I only know that girls can have them because I saw them in porn," I said.

This time, Kevin didn't hesitate. "Can I try to give you one?'

Knowing I couldn't hide the heat flaming up my cheeks, I returned his gaze. A small wave of guilt rose and fell inside my chest. Christina wouldn't be home for hours, and I'd already betrayed her with the blowjobs and the party with her husband's friends. A part of me felt that I owed Kevin something for helping me to escape and giving me a place to stay. All the years I'd fantasized about leaving the Amish were shadowed by the fear of being alone, and Kevin had saved me from that. He was the first man in my life to offer me an emotional connection at a time when I had no idea what a healthy emotional connection should feel like.

"Okay," I said and followed Kevin to their bedroom, excited about possibly having my first orgasm.

Kevin helped me out of my clothes and slid off my thong panties, which I was still fond of wearing. I gasped as he rolled his tongue around my clit and put his finger inside me. Part of me felt ready to explode, but I still couldn't let go. Kevin lifted his head to catch his breath and said,

"You have to relax." He continued, but I couldn't orgasm.

"I have an idea," he said. "Have you ever played with a vibrator?"

"No, what's that?"

"It helps women have orgasms." He pulled a vibrator out of Christina's dresser drawer; it was about eight inches long and an inch thick.

"How does it work?" I asked.

"This button turns it on." He pressed it and let me feel the vibrations with my hand.

I wrapped my fingers around it, imagining the pulsating inside me. "That looks fun."

I threw myself back on the bed and covered my face with a pillow. Kevin touched the vibrator to my clit and moved it around slowly. My legs began to shake, and an intense buildup released and shot through my whole body. I lost control and let out a scream as my body quivered, and I had my first orgasm. My body was still pulsating as I lay there with my eyes closed, enjoying a feeling of euphoria I had never felt before.

Christina had no idea what Kevin and I were up to. Having sex with Kevin made me feel naughty and alive. But I was young and naive. He kept assuring me that he'd divorce Christina one day so we could be together. I didn't understand back then that I was being groomed; how young and impressionable I really was; and how lost I was in my pursuit of freedom.

I became increasingly lonely living at Tammy's house. I told Kevin I couldn't take it anymore, so he drywalled the storage room in the back of their house and turned it into a bedroom. I was so happy to live with them finally. Most days I was still alone, but they had a trampoline to jump on and dogs to play with, which helped pass the time, and I enjoyed spending the evenings with them.

Then Kevin introduced me to Frank, who started coming over on weekends to have coffee while Christina was away doing errands. They invited me to join them and flattered me with compliments. I was so cool and different from other girls because I was "easy to get along with," they said.

Kevin began boasting to Frank about how he'd had sex with me and how good I was at giving blowjobs. "Frank's wife hasn't had sex with him since his last kid was born," Kevin said. "I bet he could use a good blowjob."

I stayed quiet, shocked that Kevin would suggest such a thing. Frank turned bright red and wouldn't look me in the eye. The next time he came over, though, he asked Kevin if he could take me into the bedroom. Kevin agreed, and I thought, "Why not?" I gave Frank a blowjob. He was in his sixties and couldn't get hard, but still orgasmed. His saggy balls grossed me out. I did it because it made him so happy, which, at the time, made me feel better about myself.

After that, Frank stopped by periodically while I was home alone to get his blowjob. He often gave me twenty bucks afterward. I didn't know about prostitution back then. I just thought he was being nice. We tried to have sex, but he couldn't get a full erection. Again, I knew it was wrong, but I couldn't resist the feeling I got when I was being naughty and keeping a secret. Kevin and Frank spoke so highly of me afterward, which made me feel special and important.

Kevin told me that English girls shave their pubic hair and recommended I do the same. I found it odd that a girl would shave down there. Nevertheless, I decided to try it. At first, it felt awkward because I hadn't seen my bare lips since I hit puberty. As I lay in my bed that night, I couldn't stop touching my softly shaven lips. They felt so silky and smooth. At last, I understood why the English girls shaved. Happily, I felt more English.

Frank took a particular interest in me. Like Kevin, he masked his inappropriate sexual attraction with the promise of protection and concern for my well-being. "Kevin and Christina are too controlling," he said one day. "You might as well still be Amish. They won't even let you get a job. You're almost eighteen and should have your freedom."

I poured him some more coffee, grateful for his guidance. "Well then, you could teach me how to drive your truck," I suggested.

Frank laughed. "We can start right now." He threw me his keys, and I caught them.

Frank adjusted the seat of his pickup and showed me how to work the pedals. He hopped in beside me and put his hand over mine, turning the key in the ignition. The truck started, and I jumped, feeling the roar of the engine shoot through my legs. Driving made me feel even more independent and footloose. I couldn't wait to get my license.

As an Amish girl, I was fascinated by Christmas trees and lights. During the holidays, I would stand by the kitchen window and watch the twinkling lights of the neighbors' decorations. I fantasized about having my own tree and lights. Amish only celebrate Christmas as the birth of Christ. On the occasional Christmas Eve, "Santa" left presents on our plates: a handkerchief, salt and pepper shakers, a dish, or a coloring book. Those gifts were practical, and I felt grateful for each one.

My first English Christmas was magical. Kevin and Christina put up a beautiful tree, and I sat next to it each day, wondering if I was dreaming. I felt awkward and curious about what could be in all those presents under the tree on Christmas morning. Eventually, I gave in and had fun. Every gift was thoughtful and chosen to help make my English life easier.

In January, three ex-Amish cousins came to visit and invited me to drive to Ohio to visit other ex-Amish relatives. There, I met my second cousin, Noah, a truck driver who agreed to let me accompany him on a four-day run to New York, Boston, Connecticut, and Pennsylvania. I'd never been outside of Michigan, and it was a great experience. But an even better experience was waiting for me back in Ohio. As soon as I returned from my first road trip, I met Aaron.

# CHAPTER FOUR

My cousins took me out bowling one Friday night, where we met up with some other boys who'd been raised Amish and left as teenagers. I noticed Aaron right away. He was cute and charming and close to my age. I liked his mustache and cropped brown hair, slightly spiked on top with gel. He wore Wrangler jeans, a button-down shirt, and cowboy boots. He paid close attention to me, leaning in to share a sarcastic remark or witty commentary. It felt nice to be liked by an English boy my age who understood my past.

He called my cousin's house the next day to ask me out. We talked a bit and I felt shy. I really wanted him to like me. He was just as confident and charismatic as he was the night before. He asked if I had a boyfriend, and I said no.

"Would you like to have one?" He laughed. "Just kidding. Can I take you out to eat?"

From the moment he picked me up, Aaron was a gentleman. When we approached his red pickup truck, he opened the door and closed it behind me. When we got to Applebee's for dinner, Aaron parked and then leaned over and kissed me on the cheek. I got super flushed and excited.

After dinner, we went to the movies, where we held hands and kissed. I'd never been to a movie theater before, and it was almost as exciting as making out. Aaron asked if I wanted to go to his place. He had a bedroom in a trailer which he shared with his two brothers. I said yes.

Aaron was gentle, and I felt more liberated than ever. Finally, I was having sex with my own guy who wasn't committed to someone else. But I wanted more than sex. With Aaron, I wanted a relationship.

We sat on his bed, and I felt his eyelashes flutter against my face as he kissed me. His tongue was soft and slow, unlike Kevin's rough, demanding mouth. It seemed to wrap itself around my entire soul, and I found myself stretching my hips toward him. Aaron slowly unbuttoned my blouse, unhooked my bra, and let my bare breasts fall into his hands. He cupped them, exploring the smooth skin with his fingers before bending his head to trace my nipples with his tongue. Closing my eyes, I threw my head back and moaned. This was very different from the English boys in the cornfield.

He gently pushed me onto the bed, took off my jeans, straddled my body, and then unbuckled his belt. His cock was already straining against the fabric of his blue boxers, but only for a moment before Aaron kicked them off, lowered himself to meet me, and used his hand to help guide his erect penis inside me. Once he was in, he began slowly rotating his hips. Desire enveloped me as his erection grew larger and harder. The faster his thrusts became, the more I wanted. I pulled my legs up higher and wider, begging him not to stop. Before I was ready, Aaron's moans reached a crescendo, and the rocking slowed. No orgasm for me that first time, but I didn't care. I'd finally met someone who didn't treat me like a sex object.

For the next three weeks, Aaron and I were inseparable. I finally had a taste of what it was like to have a real boyfriend, someone my age who liked me for me. Aaron did all the things I fantasized that a real boyfriend would do. When we went places together, he held my hand; he kissed me in public. He stood behind me and wrapped his arms around my waist. He always let others know we were together. It wasn't a secret like when I was Amish or with Kevin. I didn't have to hide. For the first time, I felt content without the secrets that had driven my decisions for so long.

I wasn't ready to part with Aaron, but I wanted to leave Ohio. I was falling for Aaron, but I felt conflicted about Kevin. Even though he was married, I felt guilty, as if by being with Aaron, I was somehow cheating on Kevin. I didn't know how I'd tell Kevin I didn't want sex with him anymore. In my heart, I knew my confusion didn't make sense.

Aaron drove me back to Michigan, where he met Kevin and Christina. They seemed to approve, although Kevin made it clear he expected our sexual relationship to continue between Aaron's visits every other weekend.

After two more agonizing weeks apart, Aaron and I reunited on the sofa in Kevin and Christina's living room. Christina's rules dictated that Aaron would sleep on the couch and me in my bed, as she would not tolerate us sleeping together unmarried under her roof. Kevin nodded in agreement, as he always did in front of his wife.

Once they were asleep, I snuck into the living room and crawled onto the couch with Aaron. We pulled the blanket up over our heads to muffle our nervous giggles. Then he silenced me with his lips, kissing me hungrily and holding me close. I was thrilled to be in his arms again. Aaron quickly wiggled out of his boxers and positioned himself between my legs. At my first murmur of pleasure, he tossed me a pillow, and I pressed it into my face to muffle the sounds of my climax. I bit down into the soft fabric as he brought me to orgasm with his tongue. Then he slid his erect cock inside my wet vagina, exhaling his warm breath into my neck as he came.

Afterward, as we lay there, our naked bodies entwined in the dim light, Aaron looked into my eyes. "I love you," he whispered.

My heart fluttered with pure joy. I'd waited so long for this moment. In his arms, I felt safe, loved, and free. "I love you, too."

It was settled. Now we were officially boyfriend and girlfriend. On the weekend, we did normal boyfriend-girlfriend stuff like exploring the woods on snowmobiles and sleds and going out to eat. Every other weekend could never come fast enough and always ended too soon. Sometimes we visited with friends and cousins and went bowling or played pool. Kevin and I continued to fool around only because I didn't know how to say no to him. He insisted that Christina withheld sex from him, and I felt I owed him. Thankfully, Aaron decided he wanted to be with me full-time. He justified it by calculating that he could make more money working near Gladwin than at the sawmill back in Ohio. He wanted to be a successful business owner someday, buy a house and have a family.

That spring, Kevin got Aaron a job in Detroit, helping him remove old railroad tracks. Kevin and Aaron left on Monday mornings and returned on Friday nights, so it still felt like a long-distance relationship. I wanted to spend every minute of every day with Aaron. My heart felt so heavy when he was gone.

We finally bought a little trailer and set it up in Kevin and Christina's backyard. I loved living in it and having our own little place on the weekends. It was tiny but romantically cozy with brown wood paneling and cabinets in the kitchen, and a bedroom over the fifth wheel where the ceiling stooped too low for us to stand. Our bed comforter, white with light blue flowers, matched the shower curtain in the bathroom. The kitchen had a microwave, stove, and sink; in the dining/living area, we had a sofa and a small table that turned into an extra bed. Most weekends, we didn't do much except sleep, cuddle, and have sex because Aaron left early on Monday mornings to go back to Detroit for the week.

After receiving several letters from family members urging me to visit, I decided it was time, hoping the relief at finding me alive and well would overshadow their shock of seeing me English. That spring, Christina drove me a half hour back to my parents' house and waited in the car as I knocked on the door. It was just after lunchtime and my siblings jumped up from the table and crowded around the door and windows, clamoring to get a glimpse of me. My mom stood in the doorway with my dad behind, the screen door still closed between us.

"You can't come in dressed like that," Mom said, wiping away a tear.

I looked past her at my dad, silently pleading with him to reconsider. When his eyes darted away, I could see the tears he was trying to hide, and it hit me how much my leaving had hurt him. I'd never seen my dad cry before. It broke me. I cried, too, because I missed them, and I realized that nothing would ever be the same between me and my family.

"Fine," I said. "I'll just go, I guess." As I turned to walk back to the car, I heard the screen door creak open.

I was allowed to come in. I stayed for over an hour, talking mostly to my younger siblings, who were now four, six, seven, and eight years old, and crowded around me asking questions. Dad stood in the corner with a disappointed expression and didn't say much. After I said goodbye to my siblings, my parents pulled me aside and Dad said, "You don't have to burn in Hell. You can still be saved if you come home."

I was unsure if he actually missed me or if he was distraught because he thought I was going to hell. Or was he grieving his reputation as a good Amish father in the eyes of the church and God? When I left, everyone gathered at the doors and windows again. I watched them stare at us until Christina turned back onto the road and they faded away into the distance.

Kevin and Christina threw me my first birthday party when I turned eighteen. I was so excited because the Amish don't celebrate birthdays! Aaron was there with his brother, along with many of my ex-Amish cousins and some of our English neighbors. Kevin cooked hamburgers and hot dogs on the grill, and Christina bought me my first birthday cake decorated with a horse theme and candles. Aaron gave me a necklace and a black leather jacket with burgundy fringe. I felt like a child, filled with joy and gratitude, but I couldn't wait for Monday. I was finally old enough to get my driving permit. Being eighteen also meant I could get a job. Total freedom was so close!

Christina took me to the DMV on Monday morning to get my permit and fill out an application at Burger King. I got hired and started the following week. Having my driving permit and a job made me feel English. I was so happy to have my own money because I'd no longer be dependent on Kevin and Christina.

In August, a friend of Aaron's offered him a job at a roofing company in Minnesota. Aaron wanted to move, and I was thrilled. We said goodbye to Kevin and Christina and the little trailer. Christina hugged me and assured me I could always come back. As she said goodbye to Aaron, Kevin helped me fit the last suitcase into the back of Aaron's truck. He seemed to want to say something, but Christina and Aaron were too close. I was glad. I wanted to put him and Frank and Christina's vibrator and the fuzzy memories behind me. I turned my back to him and got into the passenger seat as Aaron climbed in beside me. "Ready?" he asked.

Kevin and Christina were waving from their doorway. I could see them in the periphery of my vision, but I never looked back at them. I looked straight at Aaron. "I've never been more ready."

Three days after we moved to Minnesota, a loud knocking on the front door woke us at six in the morning.

"It's the police! Open the door or we're kicking it in!"

I thought it was someone pretending to be the police and trying to break in. Scared, I started to cry.

"What's going on, Aaron?"

He said not to worry. It was the police. We were sleeping on an air mattress in the living room because we didn't have our bed yet. Aaron answered the door in his boxers. One of the officers announced that he had a warrant for his arrest, read him his rights, and handcuffed him.

"Please don't hurt him," I cried. The officer said Aaron was under arrest and had to go with them.

"Don't take him away," I begged. "I just moved here and don't know anyone." The officer ignored me. "Aaron, what happened?" I asked.

"I'll explain later," he said. "Call Becky, John's wife. Her number's on the fridge."

I nodded. I'd just met them the day before. Aaron asked the officer if he could at least put on pants. I couldn't stop crying; I was so scared and confused. Why would Aaron bring me to Minnesota if he knew he might go to jail?

I called Becky and she explained that Aaron had failed to pay some traffic tickets from several years back. He'd likely have to post bail to get out of jail and then pay the fines to avoid more jail time. By noon, Aaron posted bail and I picked him up.

"I'm sorry I didn't tell you," he said as I drove him home. "I planned on telling you, but I didn't think the police would find me so quickly."

I was thrilled to see him and grateful he didn't have to do any more jail time, so I decided to make the best of our move to Minnesota despite the rough start.

Aaron introduced me to his friends, Eli and Tina, both of whom I'd known when I was Amish. I told Tina I needed a job, and she recommended I apply at a nearby factory. Sure enough, they hired me. For a few months, I worked on the assembly line, where my job was to hang parts on a line to be painted. Once they were painted, I had to put them in a box. Time became static and dull, and I quickly got bored by the monotonous routine. Then a co-worker announced he was leaving for IBM. I asked him what IBM was, and he explained it was a big company that made computer parts and paid good money. So, I also applied and got that job, which felt like a step up. I disliked working the graveyard shift, but I put up with it because I was happy that my bank account was growing.

I expected Aaron to be affectionate, loving, and cuddly all the time, like he was when we lived in Michigan. Instead, living in Spring Valley, Minnesota, he seemed bored with me, and we grew apart. Then Aaron's first cousin moved into the second bedroom so she could save money. Mary was five-foot-four and 115 pounds with dark eyes accentuated by lots of makeup and shoulder-length hair that she styled with a curling iron. I thought she was beautiful. Mary was also ex-Amish and worked as an exotic dancer. She never told me directly, but she left for work in the afternoons dressed in miniskirts and halter tops and returned in the middle of the night. Fishnet stockings and lingerie hung over our shower rack to dry. She also commanded a lot of Aaron's attention. I'd sometimes walk into the apartment to find them whispering only to stop when they saw me. She made flirtatious remarks, which Aaron returned. They talked and laughed together while I stayed silent, not knowing what to say or how to chime in. I could tell they were flirting, which made me super insecure and jealous.

Looking back, I realize they were probably talking about Mary's work and the guys she encountered, but I couldn't read between the lines because I knew nothing about strip dancing. Over the eight months Mary lived with us, I became convinced Aaron was cheating on me with her. Aaron and I argued about it, and he reminded me that they were first cousins. "I would never have sex with my cousin," he argued. He accused me of being jealous of her and assured me I had no reason to be. I didn't believe him and was relieved when she moved out.

Things went back to normal for a few months, but then Aaron started coming home late from work. Again, I suspected him of cheating. I confronted him, but he denied it, accusing me of trying to push him away. We began arguing a lot. One night, I was waiting for him at the door.

"Where were you?" I cried. "Who are you seeing?"

Reaching into his front pocket, Aaron flung an engagement ring at me. "Are you happy now?" he yelled. My jaw dropped. He asked me to marry him, and I said yes.

Despite Aaron's shotgun proposal, the arguing continued, and he started sleeping on the couch. I didn't know what I wanted anymore. I considered going back to the Amish. I talked to Aaron about it, and he supported the idea. I think he was happy to get rid of me. So, I left my car and all my belongings in Minnesota with him. I knew in my heart that I didn't want to be Amish, but I had to do something different. Being in Minnesota with Aaron wasn't working for me.

I returned to Michigan and told my family I wanted to be Amish again. They were delighted, and I felt overwhelmed by all the attention. My mom excitedly suggested we make new dresses and *kapps* for me. When I ran away, they burned most of my Amish clothes, believing if they burned their kids' clothing after they ran away, they would get homesick and come back. I was grateful for the new dresses, but uncertain about staying. I didn't want Mom to waste her time and money.

I tried to forget Aaron and the English world, but I couldn't. A part of me wanted to go back to my English life. The rest of me wanted to be Amish. I felt trapped by the thought of being Amish for the rest of my life. I was torn between freedom and my family who loved me. I felt so unloved and alone in the English world, and it was comforting to be loved by my family. I decided to give it my all for a few days. Maybe being Amish was what I needed.

A few days later, I knew I couldn't stay. I felt incredibly guilty making my family believe I was there for good. If I left again, they'd be hurt more than they were the first time. I didn't know if I could find the strength, but I couldn't stand it. After being there for just ten days, I ran away again. I left a note and ran as fast as I could across the road into the ditch. Once I was off the main road, I ran to the English neighbors' house and asked them for a ride to town. They wanted to know what happened and why I was breathing so heavily. I told them I ran away from my Amish family for the second time. They seemed surprised and couldn't understand why I would do that, but they agreed to drop me off at Burger King. I called Kevin and Christina and asked them to please rescue me again.

I was relieved to be free again. After a few days with Kevin and Christina, I asked Aaron to pick me up and bring me to Minnesota. He agreed but told me he had a new girlfriend. I was devastated and panicked. How was I going to live without him? I thought about how I could kill myself. I loved him and thought we were going to be together forever. Never having been on my own, I felt scared and lost without him.

Kevin told me not to worry. "Don't kill yourself," he said. "Someday we'll be together."

# CHAPTER FIVE

After Aaron and I broke up, I moved into my own apartment. I'd never lived by myself before and felt unsure I could make it on my own. I became close friends with Eli's wife, Tina, and I talked to her about my worries.

"You'll be fine," she assured me.

"How do you know?" I asked. "I can hardly pay my bills."

Tina laughed. "Oh, sweetie, there are lots of ways to pay the bills."

Now, I was curious. "Like what?"

Tina lowered her voice. "I used to make lots of money dancing in Detroit."

"What kind of dancing?" I asked.

She paused before answering. "Stripping." Tina chuckled at my silence. "Does that shock you?"

I didn't answer right away, but I thought, "how could she do such a thing? Wasn't she embarrassed to take her clothes off, especially in front of strangers?"

Tina suggested we go out Friday night so I could "free my mind and feel better."

I asked where we were going, but she said it was a surprise. "You won't be disappointed," she assured me.

We pulled into the parking lot where a rotating multi-colored neon sign spun silhouettes of two curvaceous women on a pole. A huge sign welcomed us to Class Act Peelers, a nude gentlemen's club. The old building looked more like an old warehouse than a strip club.

"We're here!" Tina laughed at the look on my face. I was shocked; I couldn't believe she'd taken me to a strip club.

I was nervous but excited at the same time. I'd come to believe that strippers were sluts and bad people. I thought that I should've made it more clear to her how I felt.

As soon as we walked in, a naked woman appeared on stage. Stopping in my tracks, I gasped, and Tina grabbed my hand and led me to the bar. We sat near the far end of the stage where we could talk.

"How can they just take their clothes off like that?" I asked.

"Easy money," Tina explained. "They're probably paying their way through college or supporting whatever habits they have."

"What do you mean?" I asked. "What habits?"

Tina just smiled mysteriously.

I sat back, listening to the music and watching the dancer on stage. She was so confident, and her sexy moves intrigued me. It looked like she was having fun. I couldn't help but wonder about her. What did her parents think? Did they even know?

The song ended, and she picked up her bra and stepped off the stage. Her eyes lingered on me as she walked by. I felt a swarm of butterflies rise in my stomach. Why would she look at me like that?

Tina said she needed to use the ladies' room. I waited at the bar, taking tiny sips of ice water. I felt extremely uncomfortable and tried to relax. Closing my eyes, I encouraged myself to be open-minded. When I looked up at the new girl on stage, our eyes met, and she smiled. I felt I could never take my clothes off and dance in front of strangers, but wow, it looked like an easy way to make money. Tina returned. "So, what do you think?"

"I'm still in awe," I replied, "It looks like fun."

Tina smiled. "Dancing can be anything you make it."

A man approached me, his slicked-back hair and goatee flecked with silver, in an expensive-looking suit, and wearing an expression that identified him as someone in charge. His eyes scanned my body, and he introduced himself as Donovan, the club manager. "Your friend said you need a job."

Blushing, I looked at Tina, who just stood there with a sly smile on her face. "Oh," I stammered, "I don't think I could ever do that."

"Why not?" Donovan asked.

His eyes studied me, never breaking eye contact, even when I looked away. "I'm too shy."

"Come back to my office," he said. "I want to talk to you some more." He walked away, confident I'd follow, and I did, thinking I had nothing to lose.

Donovan sat behind the desk and motioned for me to sit facing him, then asked me where I was from and my age. Heat spread from my cheeks to my neck and fluttered into my chest as I answered his questions, assuring him I wasn't ready to take my clothes off in front of a bunch of strangers.

"You're young and beautiful," he said. "If you change your mind, you'll make a lot of money. All you need is some confidence. Guys like the shy, innocent look."

"I'm sorry," I said.

He shrugged and motioned toward the door, signaling that I could leave. "If you change your mind, let me know. We'd love to have you."

When I returned to sit with Tina at the bar, we were quickly surrounded by three dancers who introduced themselves as Taylor, Ashley, and Mercedes. They hovered around me, and Mercedes casually asked how I was doing.

"Fine," I replied. The dancers gave me a skeptical look. "I'm a little nervous," I added. "I've never been to a place like this."

They looked at each other as if they shared a secret. "It's okay," one of them reassured me, caressing my arm. "We really want to see you dance on stage."

I almost fell out of my chair. "They must be crazy," I thought.

"Why me?" I asked.

Without answering, they playfully grabbed my arms and pulled me to the dressing room with Tina close behind. One dancer pulled my shirt over my head while another slipped off my skirt. Tina held up two skimpy outfits, and they all agreed on a hot pink bikini top with matching booty shorts. I stood in front of the mirror, staring at the pink cloth barely covering my body. Tina had a big smile on her face. "Come on, my friend, you'll be fine. It's fun; just try it." The next song came on and I heard someone say, "Good luck!" Then they pushed me out the door toward the stage.

"Pour Some Sugar on Me" by Def Leppard burst through the speakers. "I'm not ready for this," I said weakly, but I took the last step onto the stage, and there was no turning back.

"Here I am," I thought. "I might as well make the most of it!" I walked to the pole, grabbed hold of it, and started shaking my hips to the music. Tears welled up in my eyes, but I blinked them away, determined not to let anyone see the terror I felt. I shook my long blond hair so it fell in front of my face, shielding me from the audience. Bending over, I swayed my hips back and forth as I'd seen the other dancers do, trying to look sexy. People clapped and threw money onto the stage. Feeling encouraged, I tilted my head and bit my lower lip as I shyly removed the bikini top and shorts. A wave of hot energy rushed through my entire body. What had I just done? My breasts were exposed for all to see. Everyone, both men and women, flocked to the edge of the stage and I felt like a rock star.

As the second song began: Def Leppard's "Love Bites," I hooked one finger beneath my panty strap and slowly tugged while bending over until the panties were lying on the floor. I stepped out of them, now completely naked and vulnerable. A moment of panic shot through me as I wondered what my Amish family would think if they could see me now, and I took a moment to pray they'd never find out. When I stepped on stage, I had crossed through a doorway from which I could never return. It felt like only yesterday that I'd worn the long, heavy dresses, aprons, and head coverings that the Amish said would prevent me from burning for eternity. It was a sin to tempt others, explore our own bodies, or acknowledge our sexuality. Everything I'd been taught promised that after tonight I was going straight to Hell.

I smiled at the cheering audience, trying to block out my emotions. I remembered Tina's seductive whisper in my ear before I went on stage: "Pretend you're having sex." I got down on my hands and knees, arched my back, and imagined Aaron making love to me, doggy style. But then I replaced his face with the man closest to the stage and pictured the tall, dark stranger taking me right there on stage with the world watching. My fantasy of a normal life with Aaron filled with bowling and matching bathroom sets was over. Instead, here I was in a strip club, crawling around like a cat in heat. Hiding my face behind my hair, I rolled onto my back and spread my legs. People screamed and cheered when I did that. I opened my eyes and it hit me that I was completely naked. I couldn't believe what I was seeing: my own vagina.

Finally, the song ended, and I gathered the money and walked back to the dressing room. Wow, what a rush! The girls gathered around me, telling me I was a natural dancer. "How do you feel?" someone asked.

"Scared," I replied, "but good." Mercedes appeared and hugged me. "Congratulations! You looked great out there. You should come back and dance again."

Before going back to the bar, I counted fifty-five dollars in tips. I was surprised at how easy it was.

Tina was waiting for me at the bar with a huge smile on her face. "Damn, girl! You rocked it. Good job."

Donovan came over to ask what I thought. Still high from the rush, I pretended to think about it for a moment. "I think I might want to work here after all."

"Great," he said. "You can start tonight."

Even though the club was an hour-and-a-half drive from my house, I started working there three days a week from four to nine p.m.; then I went to work at IBM until seven in the morning. The girls at the club began calling me Barbie because of my long blond hair, so that became my stage name. Each night, taking my clothes off got easier, and I began to relax and enjoy myself. Within a few shifts, I was hooked and couldn't believe how much money I was making. All my friends in Spring Valley kept asking what I was doing all weekend because I was never around anymore. Some of them even jokingly asked if I was a stripper, but I couldn't admit it. Tina warned me never to reveal my secret to my friends because they'd be jealous and look down on me.

Eventually, I got sick of working two jobs. I wanted to quit IBM and work at the club full-time, but Tina wanted me to have a normal life and talked me out of it. So, I kept both jobs.

It wasn't long before I started dating a customer. I wasn't over Aaron, but I was ready to move on, and when Rodney asked me out, I couldn't resist. I liked his cowboy boots, hat, Wranglers, and his devilish dark goatee. Rodney was twelve years older than me, and his maturity made Aaron seem like a kid. I was ready to be an adult. As I danced over him, he whispered that he wanted to see me ride his horse across his ranch in Michigan. I lowered myself onto his lap, intrigued. My voice came out in a husky whisper. "You have a horse?" His deep brown eyes lit up as he recognized my sudden interest, and he nodded.

We continued to talk as I shook and shimmied around him. He said he was in town on business but separated from the mother of his daughter, so I could visit him on the ranch anytime. It was a nice fantasy, but I didn't take his offer too seriously. When he came into the club again two weeks later, he asked me to go out with him after my shift. At first, I said no. Tina cautioned me never to date customers. It was just asking for trouble, she'd said. But Rodney persisted, and I couldn't resist. My pussy tingled at the thought of having sex with him. What did I have to lose? I felt safe with him. If it didn't work out, he was just one customer.

The next evening, I brought an overnight bag to work and said yes to Rodney. He waited for my shift to end, and we met up at a nearby hotel. As we waited for the elevator, Rodney rubbed my thigh and teased the edges of my garter belt through my miniskirt with his fingers. I covered the bulge in his jeans with my hand and dragged my long nails across the shape of his balls.

Once in the elevator, we couldn't wait any longer. He pinned me against the back wall and hoisted my legs around his waist. His goatee tickled my skin as he kissed me passionately, his hands grabbing my ass and his hard cock straining against his jeans. The doors opened, and we laughed as Rodney carried me to the hotel room, still wrapped around his waist. He plopped me on the couch and told me to help myself to the minibar. Then he disappeared into the bathroom, where I heard him start the bath water. A few minutes later, the door opened and he emerged, the scent of lavender wafting behind him. He led me into the hot bubble bath.

"Aren't you going to join me?" I asked.

"No, this is all for you. I'll massage your feet though, if you'd like."

"Yes, please," I said. No one had ever rubbed my feet before. I sank into the luxuriously frothy water and propped my feet on the edge. Rodney sat on the tiles next to the tub and wrapped my aching feet in his strong hands. Closing my eyes, I sank further into the warm water, arching my feet into Rodney's fingers. His hands slowly rode up my ankles and calves, sliding his skin along mine, exploring the ebb and flow of my body. The bubbles dripped over the sides of my thighs as Rodney rose to his knees and caressed my hips, then gently stroked the top of my clit with his fingertips. Touching me like he was trying to open the petals of a delicate flower, Rodney waited until I strained towards him, begging for more. He slid two fingers deep inside me, and I shuddered, splashing droplets of water over his face. In one graceful move, Rodney stood and lifted me out of the tub, dripping wet, and carried me to the bed. He'd already laid out a towel, placed me on top of it, and lovingly patted me dry. He had it all planned out, I realized. It was incredibly thoughtful and romantic.

Rodney moistened his hands with oil and massaged my thighs, moving slowly to my backside and up my spine. He spoke in a gentle voice. "How does that feel?"

I felt myself melting into the sheets, every pore in my body primed for a sexual release. "Wonderful," I murmured.

He lay down beside me and guided me to straddle his face. My bare pussy hovered over his mouth, hot and hungry for me. He reached up and gently squeezed my breasts as I lowered myself onto his waiting lips. He opened me up with his warm tongue, swirling it around. His goatee prickled the insides of my thighs as I rode his mouth until I quivered and cried out with pleasure. With his stout cock, he entered me with confidence. He lasted much longer than Aaron or Kevin ever had.

Rodney was able to control when he came. When I told him that I'd never cum during intercourse, he was shocked. I assured him that I loved sex, especially with him, but Rodney decided his new goal was to make me orgasm while he was inside me. He became in tune with my body so that he could help me relax and let go.

The next time I saw Rodney, he achieved his goal. After an hour of massage and patient foreplay, he rocked himself inside me until I felt the deep crescendo of ecstasy building inside my walls, then exploded in a wave of intense release. We had sex even more after that because I really enjoyed those orgasms.

Two months later, Rodney asked me to move to Michigan, where he lived on ten acres with his nine-year-old daughter and her horse, Lavender, a thirty-year-old retired racehorse. I'd thought a lot about moving back to Michigan after Aaron and I broke up. I said yes.

Before I moved, I asked Tina to come to the club and dance with me. She resisted, arguing that she hadn't danced in a while, but I insisted. Finally, she agreed, admitting she could use the extra money. Tina's husband, Eli, invited Rodney to stay at their house with him, and Tina and I went off to the club together. On our way out the door, Tina told them we'd stay in a hotel that night since it was such a long drive. I had no idea what she had in store for me.

When we got to the hotel, Tina pulled a marijuana joint out of her purse. "Have you ever smoked before?" she asked. I hesitated, shocked again, but admitted yes, I had tried it once but didn't like it because it made me feel paranoid.

Tina lit the end of the joint and smiled as she inhaled. "Oh, it's ok." She winked. "You're with me, we're alone in a hotel, and we're not going anywhere until morning."

She handed me the joint, and I got used to taking puffs while passing it back and forth. I began to relax.

Tina rolled onto her side to face me, a wicked grin on her face.

"Have you ever been with a girl?" she asked.

I wondered if she was out of her mind or if I had been missing out. Was she trying to corrupt me? Everything taboo was suddenly becoming a part of my reality. I was very high at this point.

Tina traced an invisible line up my arm. "I haven't been with a girl for a long time." My arm tensed beneath her finger, and she sat back, looking disappointed. "I miss it," she added. "I could have sex with you but you don't have to do anything to me if you don't want to."

Part of me felt shy, and part of me didn't want her to pull away. The look on her face made me feel like I must be missing out on something great. I felt my face melt into a huge grin and flopped back into the pillows. "Ok," I said, pointing at my pussy. I thought, "How bad could it be?" I love oral sex, and Tina had already opened my eyes and helped me to be more open and comfortable with myself.

Tina shimmied out of her clothes and straddled me. Her full breasts brushed my belly button as she leaned over and flicked my small, taut breasts with her tongue and drew each nipple into her mouth. They immediately perked up, and the rest of my body tingled with nervous anticipation. She slid her bare breasts up to meet mine and kissed me. It felt different than kissing men. Tina was more sensual and responsive to my tongue. I couldn't wait to feel her full lips on my pussy. My pelvis arched toward her mouth, and I moaned. Tina obliged and moved down to my inner thighs, tickling them with her lips and teasing me with her tongue. Her fingers glided lightly across my clit, and I shivered as she gently slipped one inside. She waited for my moaning to turn into pleading for more, more. She indulged me with a second finger, and I leaned in, desperate for her to fill the void. She did by covering my pulsing clit with her warm, soft mouth. Her skilled tongue massaged my quivering lips until I bucked against her mouth in spasms of relief.

After my orgasm, I wondered if I could give her one. She coached me, guiding my head with her hands, saying, "There … yeah just like that … mmm, good job." I loved the sensation of her smooth lips and taut clit beneath my tongue. I slid it in and around her soft, warm folds, tracing circles and figure eights as she told me. Tina guided my hands to

56

her breasts, and I gently massaged them, fingering her soft pink nipples.

Tina quickly had an orgasm, too. Afterward, I lay in her arms and thanked her for giving me these new experiences.

In the morning, I began questioning what we'd done. I thought about her husband. Would he be upset and jealous? Maybe I should've said no. On the way home, Tina could tell I was worried. She reached over from the driver's seat and ruffled my hair. "Why do you look so upset? Didn't you enjoy last night?"

"I did," I replied. "But what about your husband?"

Tina laughed. "Oh, don't worry about him. He knows I like girls, and I'm allowed to play with them."

"Are you going to tell him?"

"Of course."

I sat back, relieved, and looked out the window at the passing farmland.

"What about you?" she asked. "Are you going to tell Rodney?"

"Hmm, good question," I answered. "Probably, and if he breaks up with me, then we weren't meant to be together anyway."

As soon as we returned to Tina's place, she told the men what we'd done. Rodney's eyes lit up.

"Cool!" he said. "It sounds like the two of you had fun." He laughed and pulled me into his lap as if the idea had turned him on.

The two guys leaned over us and high-fived.

In January 2000, I moved to Rodney's home in Michigan. I didn't bring much, only some clothes, shoes, and a few sentimental items. Everything fit in the back of Rodney's truck. I said goodbye to Minnesota and moved to his double-wide trailer home on ten acres. I liked playing house with Rodney, except when his daughter came to stay on the weekends. I wasn't ready to be responsible for anyone else, let alone a nine-year-old child. Occasionally, she was with us during the week, and I'd have to drop her off or pick her up from school. But I felt jealous when she was around and resented the attention she sought from her father. What I loved most was taking care of Lavender. I spent a lot of time grooming her and learning how to ride, just as I'd fantasized about when I was a child and riding was forbidden.

I told Rodney I wanted to continue dancing, so I went to the local strip club, Sensations, to audition. Compared to the previous club, Sensations was conservative. Dancers had to wear nylons, and they didn't allow lap dances. Linda, the manager, was a grouchy, weathered-looking woman with a raspy voice who always had a cigarette dangling from her mouth. She showed me to the dressing room, where I changed into a short, skin-tight, velvet green dress and got ready to go on stage. I felt anxious again. Although I loved being on stage, my heart raced every time because I still felt vulnerable being so exposed in front of strangers. I danced for two songs as Linda sat in front, glaring at me, which made me even more nervous.

The other dancers were very welcoming. They gathered around me, asking what name I was going to use. I said I didn't know, but the girls in Minnesota called me Barbie.

A bubbly dancer named Ariel called out to me as she repaired a hole in her pantyhose. "Barbie? Girl, nobody plays with Barbie anymore. Where you from? You got a funny accent."

"I'm from Amishland," I announced.

Ariel's face lit up. "OH MY GOD SHUGA SHUGA! Sugar should be your stage name because you are so innocent. Shuga Shuga because you are so sweet."

"How do you know if I'm sweet?" I asked. "You just met me today."

"You just got that sweet look, girl," she said.

I shook my head. No one would believe my name was Sugar. "What am I gonna say when the customers ask my real name?"

"Sugar, they don't tip enough to know your real name."

All the girls insisted, so finally, I agreed and became Sugar, the new girl at Sensations.

It was fascinating to watch the other dancers perform elaborate, acrobatic pole tricks I'd never seen before. They looked so happy, graceful, and free. I also wanted to do pole tricks, so I closely watched their every move. Ariel was the best pole dancer in the club, so I asked if she'd show me how to do one of her tricks.

"The one where your back is against the pole, and you're holding onto it above your head, then pull yourself up and flip around."

"You really are crazy," she said. "That's a shoulder mount drop. Maybe you should start with something a little easier."

I insisted, and she finally agreed. I figured I had nothing to lose. Ariel made it look so easy.

"Come on then," she said. "What are you waiting for?" I walked to the pole and grabbed on but couldn't get my legs up. "Kick your legs up higher," she instructed. "And grab the pole with your legs."

Yikes, it was harder than I thought! I was unable to grab the pole with my legs. I fell on my stomach and lay on the floor, gasping for air. Ariel laughed. "I told you so. Come on, get up. You need to try again, or you'll always be afraid."

I knew she was right, so I kept trying, and it became my favorite pole trick. People looked amazed when I did it, and I learned many more. I loved pole dancing. It made me feel free. At Sensations, instead of giving lap dances, after we got off stage, we walked around the floor topless for six more songs, doing mini dances for the customers. We put our bare breasts close to their faces, then turned around and did a little booty shake. The guys tipped anywhere from a dollar to five dollars. On weekends, if I hustled, I could make three hundred to five hundred dollars a night. I planned on going to college and only dancing until I graduated. Some of the girls had been dancing for ten or more years, and I wondered why they hadn't found another job.

I became bored and unhappy living at Rodney's ranch, so I started looking for a horse to buy. I'd always wanted one and thought maybe it would keep me occupied. I found a listing in the local paper for an old white Arabian, a retired racer and show horse that needed an experienced rider. I wasn't experienced, but I told Rodney about the horse. He warned me that an Arabian's fiery temperament might be too much for me, but I convinced him we should at least have a look. So, we did—and met

Prince, who nodded his head when offered a treat. I felt magical riding Prince and ended up buying him that night.

Prince and I started competing and won a lot of ribbons. Finally, I had the white horse I always wanted. Even so, I felt unfulfilled. I wondered if the material possessions I'd coveted in the English world would ever make me happy.

I decided to buy another horse, a black, untrained Arabian named Chance. He was beautiful and wild but malnourished. As soon as I saw him, I knew he needed a new home so he wouldn't starve to death. Chance resisted my attempts to tame him, but eventually, I was able to compete with him, too. At one competition, I was warming him up with a few laps around the field when a white plastic bag began skipping alongside us in the wind. I knew Chance would get scared, so I tried to go the other way, but the bag was blowing too fast. Sure enough, Chance got spooked and started bucking like a bronco. I held on tight as he reared and kicked. I couldn't control him! Finally, I flew off his back. Thankfully, I wasn't hurt and was able to catch him. Eventually, he calmed down, and we won some ribbons.

I also dreamed of having a big truck and needed something to pull my horse trailer, so I started saving money. I had no credit established, and most of my tips were in one- and five-dollar bills. Before long, I'd saved forty bundles of one-dollar bills for a total of four thousand dollars and found a used truck for sale, and took Rodney with me to the dealership. I handed the loan officer all forty rolls of bills. He looked at me like I was crazy. "I can't accept cash like that."

I was confused because I thought he'd be happy to get all that cash. But they wanted a cashier's check. I really wanted that truck, so I went to the bank, got the check, and drove the truck home the same day. That truck was my baby. I tinted the windows and got bigger tires and a dual exhaust, so it was louder and cooler. I even put a decal of grazing horses in the back window. Finally, I felt like a real cowgirl.

Even though I was in love with Rodney, I wasn't ready for a relationship with his daughter. I was twenty-one, immature, and felt jealous when she was around. When his daughter visited on weekends, she insisted on sleeping in the bed with us and sitting between us in the truck.

I needed a break from Rodney, so I rented a bedroom and horse stall from a couple I met through horse competitions. Jeff and Tracy were in their fifties, and they both drove semi-trucks for the U.S. Postal Service. Each night, Tracy made dinner, Jeff made popcorn, and we watched movies together. In the mornings, I fed their horses along with my own.

Rodney wanted to work things out, but I was done with him. Prince, Chance, and I had a home where we were comfortable, and Jeff and Tracy became a big influence in my life. They couldn't have kids, so they treated me like their own daughter and encouraged me to start college. While living with Rodney, I completed my GED and was now ready to sign up for college courses.

I was so excited to go to college. I began with four classes, even though Tracy suggested I start with two, until I got used to the work requirements. I was stubborn and determined, and I didn't believe her. Soon, I discovered that college was not so easy. I never had homework in Amishland. I tried to manage my full-time job, college classes, and my two horses, but it was difficult.

I was making good money and wanted to live closer to school, so I decided to look for my own apartment and continue boarding my horses with Jeff and Tracy. They wanted me to stay but said they supported whatever choice I made. I was still undecided when Tracy introduced me to her nephew. Justin was tall and handsome with beautiful dark brown eyes, dark hair, a goatee, and tattoos. He was also a convict who'd just completed a prison sentence, but Tracy believed her nephew had turned his life around and learned his lesson and thought I'd be a good influence on him. Her one rule was no unmarried sex in her home. As soon as I laid eyes on him, I knew I needed to move out.

I had no idea that Justin would be a gateway to everything my parents had warned me about. Justin was the deceptively dark current just beyond the bend of the river, past the line of sight from the safety of my mother's garden and the protective arms of my father. Justin was that part of the river that looks inviting from a distance, but once you're in it, snatches you up and carries you far, far away.

# CHAPTER SIX

Justin was a bad boy. His swagger alone gave me butterflies. So, I didn't mind that his idea of a first date was spending the night with him after I got off work. I packed an overnight bag and could hardly wait for my shift to end. At two o'clock in the morning, I was exhausted and dreading the hour-long drive, but as soon as I started the truck, I got a burst of energy, tingling with excitement as I revved the engine and pushed the speed limit.

Justin greeted me outside the house—a big, fancy manufactured home that belonged to his dad and stepmom. I ran to him and wrapped my legs around him as we kissed. He carried me around the side of the house, through a door that led to his basement apartment straight to his bedroom. He lowered me onto the king bed and pulled my shirt over my head. As he reached for my bra, I gently held out my arm to slow him down. "I need to shower first," I said.

Justin sat back, pouting a bit. "Are you sure? I already waited all night for you."

"I'm sure. I feel dirty from dancing and working."

He sighed but then jumped up to turn on the shower. "Then that's what we'll do."

I followed him into the bathroom, where he watched me undress and step under the warm water. Then he followed me in. I felt so kinky taking a shower with Justin. He pressed me against the wall and kissed me as the water trickled over my breasts and dripped down my thighs, and then he gently nudged me to my knees. He had the tiniest penis I'd ever seen.

Justin groaned when I touched the tip with my tongue. It was easy to fit all of him in my mouth. I quickly brought him to orgasm before pulling him out of the shower and into his bedroom for my turn. Despite his small size, I was really turned on. Sprawled out on his bed, I reached for his hand and guided him to touch the soft, wet lips waiting for him below. I moaned as he slipped two fingers inside me. He kissed me, exploring my breasts with his other hand. My moaning got louder as I came closer and closer to orgasm. I arched my body into him and climaxed.

When I opened my eyes, Justin had a huge grin on his face. Satisfied, he stretched and ruffled my hair. We didn't have intercourse that night, and Justin admitted that he preferred blowjobs. In turn, he was good with his mouth. Secretly, I missed the feeling of having a big cock inside me, but I liked Justin a lot.

We were lying in bed cuddling and talking when he reminded me that his dad, stepmom, and thirteen-year-old half-brother were sleeping upstairs.

"They probably heard you moaning," he said.

I gasped, mortified. "Oh no! Why didn't you tell me to be quiet?"

"Because you were enjoying yourself, and I didn't want to interrupt you."

Suddenly, I could hear how quiet and still the house was, and I felt embarrassed. "Should I leave?"

"No," he assured me. "My stepmom doesn't like me anyway, so I don't care."

I left early in the morning, heavy with guilt. I'd only met his dad briefly and never met his stepmom or brother, and I hoped it would stay that way.

I finally moved into my own apartment. It wasn't fancy, but I was proud to finally have my own place. It was right across the street from the college, so I could walk to class. I loved my new independence. However, Justin wasn't very good to me. He lied about little things. Even so, I really wanted to be with him.

I knew he worked at a factory and made decent money there, but I couldn't figure out how he paid for the expensive watches and electronics he was always buying for himself. I didn't ask. I wanted him to feel he could confide in me and decided to play it cool. Justin went to a lot of parties but insisted I stay home because he didn't want to be a bad influence. That made me even more determined to go because he was restricting me from something.

Finally, I broke down and asked him. "What's going on at these parties that makes them so forbidden? What are you hiding?"

"Trust me," he said, getting another beer from the refrigerator before heading out. "I'm not hiding anything. I'm protecting you." The screen door slammed behind him.

I watched him walk through the tall grass toward his truck. "I don't need protecting!" I called after him.

Finally, Justin gave in and took me to a party. It was packed, and right away, I noticed people coming up to Justin and whispering in his ear before they all excused themselves to go to the bathroom. When they came back, they looked nervous. I asked Justin what all those people were doing in the bathroom. At first, he avoided the question, but finally, he told me.

"They're doing cocaine. Nothing for you to worry about."

That's when I realized where he made all his money: selling drugs. I knew nothing about drugs, but I wanted entrance to this secret club he was in. I cozied up to him, smiling at him in a way I knew he liked. "I want to try some."

He pushed me away. "No!"

"Please," I begged. "Why not?"

Justin shook his head. "I don't want you to ruin your life because you have too much going on for yourself."

Once again, he denied me something, making me more curious, and

I kept bugging him. I didn't even know what cocaine was; I just wanted to try it because I felt I was missing out. I was also drunk. "You're being unfair," I snapped.

Eventually, he gave in, and I tried cocaine for the first time. I wasn't sure how I was supposed to feel, but suddenly I didn't feel drunk anymore. Full of energy, I was ready to dance, wondering why I'd I never tried this before. I felt euphoric, on top of the world, and indestructible. I stayed awake all night.

The next day, I went to my friend Andrew's house for lunch, still wired from the night before. At first, his parents were thrilled to have such an enthusiastic guest.

"What's with you?" Andrew asked when we had a moment alone.

"I didn't sleep at all last night," I whispered back.

"Aren't you exhausted?" he asked.

I shook my head. "It's the opposite. I feel so alive."

We sat down at the table with his parents, and as his mother scooped food onto my plate, she asked, "Are you always this chipper?"

"No," I said, taking a bite of her baked chicken. "I was up all night doing cocaine."

Andrew had just taken his first bite, too, and I thought he was going to throw up right there at the table. He took a gulp of water as his parents sat there speechless. "Let's talk about it after lunch, okay?" he mumbled. His parents didn't say another word. They looked really upset.

Afterward, Andrew pulled me aside. "Hey, Naomi, I'm worried about you. Are you getting into trouble?"

I didn't understand what the big deal was. I felt fine. "Don't worry about me," I assured him.

Andrew shook his head. "Cocaine is a bad drug, Naomi. Promise me you won't hang out with those people anymore."

Gently pushing him away, I said, "Andrew, I left the Amish because they were too controlling. Please don't do that to me."

I didn't know then that maybe I should have listened to Andrew.

A few months into my relationship with Justin, I came home from work to find a man sitting on the floor next to my refrigerator with a tourniquet tied around his arm. A spoon, lighter, and needle lay on the floor. His skin looked yellow; he was drooling and moaning. I was terrified he was going to die on my kitchen floor.

I immediately called Justin. "There's a man dying in my apartment!"

"Oh, that's just Ryan," Justin said casually. "I forgot to tell you he was coming by. He'll be okay."

"He needs to go to the hospital!" I yelled.

"No, he can't," Justin insisted. "There's a warrant for his arrest."

"Great!" I said, "I have a fugitive in my apartment."

Justin assured me that Ryan was high on heroin and would fall asleep soon. I left Ryan there and went to watch TV because I realized there was really nothing I could do. Every so often, he'd ignite the lighter to the bottom of the spoon until his drugs began to sizzle, then shoot them into his arm through the needle. He'd doze off again, then wake up swearing and screaming and wondering where all his drugs were. After a few hours, I convinced him to rest in the guest room, where he slept for two days straight. On the third day, I woke him up. He casually gathered his belongings and thanked me for letting him stay. Then he walked out the door as if nothing had happened.

I started coming home from work on the weekends to find Justin and his friends partying. Sometimes they didn't leave until early in the morning. One night, we were getting ready for bed when we heard banging on the door. I grabbed Justin's arm. "Someone's trying to break in!"

Justin told me to lock myself in the bedroom, and I heard him open the front door and talk to someone. Creeping back to see who it was, I hardly recognized Ryan, bleeding from pieces of glass stuck in his forehead, arms, and hands.

"Please," he begged. "Don't ask questions." He stumbled to the bathroom. About an hour later he came out, still bleeding but free of glass.

The blood still trickling down his scalp made me cringe. "You need to go to the hospital and get stitches," I said.

"No way," Justin said. "He's wanted, remember?"

"High-speed chase," Ryan explained. "I was trying to outrun the cops."

"What'd you do?" Justin asked.

"I flipped the car and went through the windshield, so I ran here."

I looked at Justin. "The cops will probably follow the blood trail he left and find him here."

"Nah," Ryan said. "It happened in the sticks somewhere, so it'll be a while before they figure it out."

Justin cleaned up the blood in the parking lot and on the stairs outside so the neighbors wouldn't get suspicious. I couldn't sleep at all. Ryan's drama felt like sheer madness. Ryan left in the morning, and I never saw him again.

With my relationship feeling increasingly unstable, I threw myself into work. I loved working at Sensations. As the months passed, I became more confident. As soon as I hit the stage, I could scan the audience and pick out my clientele, and become the center of their world, the key to their instant gratification. In those moments, they lived for me, and I reveled in the power of fulfilling all their wildest fantasies. In turn, they showered me with the attention and validation I craved.

Dan was one of my regulars. Shy, polite, and in his sixties, Dan admitted he was still a virgin. He came to the club to hang out with me, watched me dance, and tipped me to sit with him at his table. Every Thursday, he brought me flowers. I loved flowers and wanted to keep them, but I couldn't make Justin jealous by taking them home, so I threw them into the dumpster after work. All the girls knew I was Dan's favorite. He bought most of the furniture for my apartment, delivered it to Sensations, then loaded it into my truck so I could take it home. The other dancers said I was the luckiest girl ever. I didn't understand why he was so generous to me. I never went anywhere with him outside the club.

A few months later, I began to suspect that Justin was cheating on me. He'd tell me he was going away for the weekend with his buddies, but he never answered his phone and seemed distant when he returned. Casually, I asked his best friend, Ethan, if Justin was seeing someone else. Ethan confirmed that Justin was seeing "a crackhead named Layla."

I sighed heavily, fighting the urge to cry. I didn't know what a crackhead was, but it confirmed that Justin was cheating.

I'd heard the term "crackhead," but I had no idea what it meant. I didn't know about crack cocaine yet.

That night, when Justin let himself into my apartment with his key, I snatched it out of his hand. "It's over," I told him. He didn't put up much of a fight. Justin was never really into me. I just wanted him to be.

Even though our relationship was ending, my relationship with the drugs Justin introduced me to was just beginning. After the breakup, I started bringing Dan's flowers home. Right away, Dan asked why I stopped throwing away his flowers. My heart felt like it might drop right out of my chest.

"How did you know?" I asked.

Dan smiled reassuringly, the way he always did, so I wouldn't feel bad when I slighted him. "It's okay. I was usually still in the parking lot when you left for the night, and I saw you throw them away. I knew you had a boyfriend, so I understood why you didn't take them home."

Humbled by his kindness, I asked, "Why did you keep bringing me flowers if you knew?"

"Because I saw how happy you were when I gave them to you."

Dan was a very sweet man, but I was mildly creeped out at the time because it felt a little like he was stalking me.

After Justin, I was lonely, and when a customer named Todd asked me to hang out with him after my shift, I reluctantly agreed. Todd was close to my age and cute, with spiked brown hair and brown eyes, but I quickly realized that our energy and personalities didn't match up for dating. Hanging out with him was awkward because his character was so dry, and we didn't have much in common besides the club. But Todd did cocaine, my new favorite drug, thanks to Justin, and he was generous with it. He explained that he came from a rich family and admitted he was spoiled. Of course, he complained about everything.

On a Saturday evening, Todd called me at work to invite me over, and when my shift ended, I drove to a gated community in the wealthiest part of town where he lived with his parents. He showed me around their mansion with a pool and a hot tub out back, but I didn't pay much attention. I couldn't take my eyes off his friend, Rowan.

Rowan was tall, witty, and charismatic, with brown hair and green eyes. He smiled easily and showered me with compliments. After a few lines of cocaine, the three of us ended up in Todd's bed.

Todd sprawled out on his back as I straddled him and lowered my naked body to his lips. He wrapped his arms around my thighs and pulled me down, consuming my clit with his mouth. Rowan kneeled in front of me, and I unzipped his pants and freed his cock. Rowan had the biggest dick I'd ever seen. I was excited to ride it but wondered if it would fit inside me. Todd couldn't stay hard and went off to do more lines, so it was just Rowan and me. I cautioned him, pointing out how big he was.

"You be on top so you can control how deep I go," he suggested. Excited and nervous all at the same time, I climbed on top of him and slowly slid him a few inches inside me. I was dripping wet and ready to go. For a moment, I hovered there, feeling every inch stretch inside me. It felt amazing. I slowly slid up and down and rocked back and forth. Rowan gripped my hips with his hands, guiding me faster, and then harder.

"Just a little more. Don't stop!" I begged.

Gently kissing my neck, Rowan stood up, positioned himself behind me and caressed my nipples. Then he bent me over and entered me from behind. "Oh yes! Just like that. I'm so close!" I moaned, then yelled out as he pounded harder and harder until my pussy pulsated. We both collapsed and let out a sigh of relief.

Quickly, I got dressed, remembering the homework I had to finish before Monday morning. Rowan and Todd tried to persuade me to stay. "I have to be responsible and do my homework before class on Monday," I insisted.

Rowan grabbed me and pulled me into his lap. "I have a great idea. I think you should go get us more coke. Then we'll go up to my friend's farm, so you can see his big tractors. After that, I promise I'll do all your homework for you."

"You're gonna do all my homework?" I asked, suspiciously. "How do I know I can trust you?"

"Oh, come on," Rowan pleaded. "You know you want to."

Honestly, I was so tired I couldn't imagine getting my homework done. More coke sounded good.

Rowan and I went back to my neighborhood to get more. Then we drove to my apartment, did a few lines, and had sex again. I suggested we stay there so I could do my homework instead of going to his friend's farm, but Rowan told me to stop worrying, assuring me he'd finish it by morning. I didn't understand the big deal with Devin's farm until we got there, and I realized Rowan just wanted to show me off. He kept telling Devin how cool I was and how much fun we'd just had. I politely watched as Devin showed me his massive tractors.

Rowan came up behind me, put his arms around my waist, and winked at his friend. "Here's your chance, brother. Don't be shy."

Devin blushed and kept showing me the details of some farm equipment as Rowan continued. "You should check out her hot body. Go ahead and touch her."

I thought he was joking. Devin's face was as red as a beet as he grinned at me shyly. "Don't worry, Devin," I said. "We're just playing around."

It was getting cold, so we went inside and played cards. Rowan kept hinting that Devin should take me to his bedroom. Finally, I had enough.

"It's not going to happen, Rowan. Clearly, Devin is shy. What makes you think I want to have sex with your friend, anyway?"

Rowan rolled his eyes. "It doesn't matter if you want to or not. You should do it because I'm trying to hook up my friend."

For a moment I was speechless. I wondered how Rowan could be such a scumbag. Devin was not attractive, with his bushy beard and barnyard aroma. Besides, I was attracted to Rowan. I looked at Devin. "Do you want to have sex with me?"

In a quiet voice, Devin said, "I prefer to take a pretty girl on a date first." I felt bad for him, and I think he was embarrassed by how Rowan treated me, but it didn't stop me from wanting to see Rowan. The coke already had a strong hold over me, so none of it mattered if Rowan kept providing it, which he did. When the lines of white powder ran out, all I could think about was getting more. Finally, at eight o'clock Sunday night, I insisted that we go back to my apartment to get my homework done. He said sure, but we needed more coke to stay up. At that point, I didn't think I had any other options. We got more, and Rowan turned on the TV. I knew then that he never planned on helping me. I felt brain-dead.

"Have you missed any school days?" Rowan asked.

"I have all A's," I said. "I haven't missed one day."

He smiled. "Perfect."

"What do you mean?" I asked.

"If you haven't missed any days and you're doing well, then you can afford to skip class tomorrow."

I was so tired. Taking the day off sounded great. I could finally relax. Besides, I had everything going for me. My truck was paid off, I had my own apartment and money in the bank, and I was in my second semester of college. It was an exciting time for me.

I skipped class.

At first, we agreed only to do drugs on Wednesdays and weekends, but before long, we were doing coke almost daily. I didn't like being around people when I was high. I missed more classes, and my instructors became concerned. I knew what I was doing was dangerous, but I couldn't stop. During the last half of the semester, I hardly ever showed up to class.

Everyone assumed Rowan and I were a couple. I had a huge crush on him, but Rowan quickly made it clear I was in the friend zone. Regardless, he occasionally indulged me. One night, we stopped at a cemetery and walked around. There was an eerie feeling as if the dead were peering at us as we walked past their graves.

"Let's go to the car and have spooky sex," Rowan suggested.

A shiver went down my spine. "I'm scared. I want to leave."

"Don't be a sissy," he whispered in my ear. "Spooky sex will be fun. Come on; you're the one that always wants to have sex."

I couldn't resist.

Rowan reclined the front passenger seat all the way, and I straddled him, my tongue wrapped around his. Like a lap dance, I began grinding on the huge bulge ready to burst through his pants. His hand entered my panties and rubbed my clit as his other hand pressed into my ass so he could grind harder. It felt so good I forgot we were in the cemetery. Shifting out of my panties, I freed his cock and tried to slide him inside.

Rowan hesitated. "Do you have a condom?"

"No, I'm on the pill. Do we need one?"

He rolled his eyes and reached into the back seat. Tearing a piece of plastic off a grocery bag, he wrapped it around his cock.

I laughed. "This is silly." The harsh plastic took some of the pleasure away, but Rowan wanted to be careful. Even so, I was so turned on and wanted to cum. "Shhh, it's okay. Kiss me," I whispered.

Rowan anchored the plastic bag at the bottom of his cock as I rode him.

"Ride it harder!" he begged.

I bounced up and down, harder and deeper. My breathing got heavier. Forgetting about the plastic, I moaned, reaching my peak and feeling jolts of euphoria through my entire body. Sweat dripped from my eyebrows.

Rowan yelled out, "Please don't stop!"

He began to throb inside me. His cum ran down my legs because the plastic couldn't contain it. We both laughed and collapsed into the seat, still entwined, until we caught our breath.

"I guess I gotta keep some condoms in my glove box just in case," Rowan said. "You should carry some with you, too."

Pulling my clothes back on, I said, "I told you I'm on the pill."

Rowan groaned as he zipped his jeans. "That's great, Naomi, but the pill doesn't protect you from sexually transmitted diseases, you know, STDs? You never heard of those in Amishland?"

"Well, no, but soon after I left, I went to a doctor to get on the pill, and that's when I first heard about them."

Rowan looked at me before starting the truck. "You know condoms are the only way to protect you from diseases, right?"

Shrugging, I searched my memory. "I think he gave me some pamphlets, but I don't remember the details."

"Well, those details are important. You can get HIV through unprotected sex, and there's no cure for that. You never got any sex education, huh?"

"No," I laughed. "No sex education in Amishland."

He shook his head as he drove away from the cemetery. "Have you ever been checked out, you know, down there?"

"The doctor I went to wanted to do a … pap smear I think it's called? I didn't want some strange man looking at my vagina, but eventually, I let him peek."

"I was a strange man when I first saw your vagina."

We laughed because he was right, but I never wanted to be intimate with the doctor. I'd gone because Christina and Kevin had insisted it was something I had to do if I was going to be sexually active. Kevin had sat me down and told me Christina had made an appointment for me. He said that getting pregnant would ruin my body and my life. "Don't end up like all those Amish women, barefoot and pregnant your whole life. You don't have to be enslaved."

I didn't want to be enslaved — just the opposite: I wanted to be free. And I went to the drug store and bought condoms, extra-large just for Rowan. Unfortunately, Rowan didn't want to have sex very often. Maybe he was having sex with someone else, or maybe it was all the drugs, but after a while, I got tired of being rejected.

# CHAPTER SEVEN

The following Thanksgiving, I planned to visit my family because it had been so long since I'd seen them. I told Rowan I was determined to go and intended to stay away from drugs the night before. Sure enough, Rowan said it was a holiday, and we should do some cocaine to celebrate. And as usual, I gave in and agreed to get one hundred dollars' worth, as long as we got some sleep. But once the drugs were gone, Rowan wanted more, and we stayed up the entire night.

I didn't feel like going anywhere in the morning, much less on a two-hour drive to see my Amish family. I felt terrible. Rowan insisted I'd be fine and recommended I take a bag of coke for the road. I told him that was insane. But I did it anyway.

As soon as I started driving, I got paranoid and wanted to throw the drugs out the window. How did I think I could hide my addiction from my family, the people who knew me best? I looked like a train wreck. They knew nothing about drugs, but they'd know something was terribly wrong. I knew I should throw the bag away, but I couldn't. Holding the bag with one hand, I tried to sniff some coke up my nose and my hand slipped off the wheel. I realized how stupid I was being. What if a cop was sitting on the side of the road? I pulled over at a rest stop to get my fix.

When I pulled into my parent's driveway, I was so tired and out of it that I barely knew what to do. I felt like turning around and going home, but I could see my family looking out the windows. There was no turning back now. "I've got this," I thought. I'll tell them I've been sick and haven't been sleeping well. I got out of the truck and went inside. My whole family was there to greet me with tears and smiles. It was after lunch already. They wanted to know why I didn't make it in time. Of course, I had lots of excuses.

My mom asked me what was wrong. "You don't look well," she said. Everyone gathered around and stared at me. I tried to stay calm while I explained I hadn't been feeling well. Mom insisted I stay there so she could take care of me, but I didn't want more attention. The whole family sat around me and asked questions, but I couldn't tell them much because I didn't want them to worry. When my sisters popped popcorn, and brought apples and blackberry juice from the basement, it felt like the good old days. My younger brothers and I went out to the barn and got the cows ready for milking. The men stayed to finish the barn chores while the women went inside and made dinner. I got to sleep in my old bed again, which felt good.

I slept well and felt like a new person the following day. My mom was extra attentive at breakfast. "You should come home," she said. "You slept well, and now you feel better."

"Thank you, Mom, but I can't just leave college and my English life behind."

She sighed and turned away, hiding her emotions. "The way you left us behind?" she said. It hurt me to see my mom in distress. I knew she missed me and blamed herself for my leaving. "Am I the reason you ran away?" she asked.

"No, Mom, of course not," I said. "There are many reasons I ran away, and I can't explain all of them." Really, the reason was I just wanted to be English and free.

I stayed for lunch but left shortly after feeling renewed. As I drove home, I kept thinking I didn't want to do drugs anymore, but in my heart, I knew I'd be weak and give in as soon as I saw Rowan.

On Friday night, Rowan and I hung out in his house doing coke, as usual. The drug filled me with energy, and it was hard to sit still. Rowan's disinterest in sex made sitting on the sofa even harder. I craved danger and excitement.

"I want to see some hookers," I said.

"Are you serious?" he asked. "What for?"

"I've never seen any. I don't want to pick one up, I'm just curious about them."

"It's dangerous at night where they hang out." Rowan smiled. "But I bet we could find drugs there."

I started to worry because I didn't want to get robbed. "I changed my mind. Let's not go."

"Oh, come on," Rowan pushed. "You're the one that wanted to go."

"I know, but I'm scared."

Rowan put his arms around me, a rare move and one I craved. "I won't let anything happen to you," he assured me.

We drove downtown and turned onto a dark side street where a group of people stood close together.

"Turn around," I said, but it was too late. They swarmed around my truck, asking us to roll down the windows. "Rowan, we need to leave. I'm scared."

Rowan kept driving. "Calm down."

He slowed down alongside a woman walking on the curb and rolled down the window. "You have anything yummy?" he asked.

The woman smiled and nodded, and Rowan said she could get in if her friends, who were still trying to swarm the truck, backed off. "What do you want?" she asked.

Rowan told her we were looking for coke, but she said she only had rock. I'd never heard of rock, but I figured I'd be fine since I was with Rowan, and he knew about this stuff. She said her name was Serena, and we could hang out with her at Budget Suites, where she lived.

"Are you sure this is safe?" I whispered to Rowan as Serena climbed into the back.

"Shh, yeah. We're just going to smoke a little, and then we'll leave."

"Smoke?" I asked. "Smoke what? Rock?"

Rowan shushed me again and told Serena to point him in the right direction.

When we arrived at her dingy motel room, Serena reached into a drawer and pulled out a dirty, broken glass pipe.

"What's the pipe for?" I asked.

Wham! Serena slapped Rowan hard across the face. "Are you serious? She's never smoked before?"

Rowan looked stunned as he rubbed his face. "I don't think so."

"You're a shitty friend," Serena said. "I'm not introducing her to this. I don't want to see a young girl's life get ruined."

"Ok, then," Rowan agreed. "Don't give her any, but she's a big girl."

Ruin my life? I wondered what the big deal was. Rowan was impatient, urging her to hurry up.

"Chill out," Serena said. "I need to take a hit first."

They took turns puffing the pipe. The smell of the burning rock made my stomach turn, but I insisted I wanted to try it.

Serena must've gotten too high to care about my future because she took a big hit from the pipe and exhaled into my mouth. I winced at the taste, then felt a euphoric head and body rush. I'd never felt anything like it. Sometimes I wish I could forget how it made me feel. I also wish I could forget the smell and taste of burning crack. But maybe it's good that I remember. It reminds me of why I never want to smoke crack again.

We stayed at Serena's motel for more than two days. I never returned to work. Soon all I cared about was getting high on crack—the need to be high overpowered my common sense. Crack took over my brain, body, and life, and I felt helpless but comfortable.

Rowan and I were buying too much crack for Serena to handle, so she introduced us to one of her dealers. Niko was a criminal, constantly in and out of jail and always on the run. But I thought he was cute, and he was more generous with his drugs once we had sex. We only had sex a few times because he was usually too high to get it up.

My addiction got worse. Every day, I hung out with Niko, smoked crack, and went down the rabbit hole deeper and deeper into a dark abyss. I'd worked at Sensations for almost four years and hardly ever missed a day until I discovered crack and stopped showing up. I never asked, but I knew Serena was hustling on the streets to sell her body for drugs. Not long after we met, we ran out of cash, and she suggested I have sex with a drug dealer in exchange for crack.

"No way, Serena," I said. I was offended and couldn't believe she'd asked me to do that. I wasn't like her, I argued. I didn't want to be a hooker. What would my family think if they found out?

Serena reminded me that it was our only option to get more rock.

"Why don't you have sex with him?" I asked.

"He requested you!"

Neither of us had any money, and all I could think about was getting high. Serena said she was doing me a favor.

I was nervous, but her friend was nice, and it didn't last long. Afterward, he handed me a big crack rock. Serena immediately snatched it from my hand and kept most of it for herself. I was too desperate to argue. All I needed in that moment was the first hit. That's what rock did to me. It rendered me completely powerless.


In the spring of 2002, I was in my second semester of college and wanted to go somewhere for spring break like the rest of my classmates. I suggested to Rowan that we go to California, and he said I was crazy because California was too far away and we should go to South Padre Island in Texas instead. I'd never heard of South Padre Island, but he made it sound like the place to go for spring break. The next task was figuring out how to pay for it.

Rowan suggested I ask Dan for the money even though I wasn't working at Sensations anymore. So, I called Dan and said I wanted to go to South Padre Island and needed money. A few days later, Dan brought me two thousand dollars in cash. I couldn't believe it. My dream was coming true. Rowan and I were on our way to Texas.

On our way out of town, we rented a car and stopped at the dealer's house, where we picked up a big rock for four hundred dollars. I was ready to hit the road, but Rowan wanted to go to Serena's, and eventually, I gave in. Rowan showed her the rock.

"Oh my God," she yelled. "Have you two lost your mind? Where did you get the money for that?"

"Naomi's got a friend with a lot of money," Rowan boasted. "She could have anything she wanted from this guy if only she would have sex with him."

I was so disgusted. I wondered why Rowan had to be like that.

"I'm ready to leave and be on vacation," I said.

"You shouldn't drive with that much crack on you," Serena said.

"See," Rowan said. "I told you. Don't worry; we'll leave when it's almost gone."

Two days later, the rock was gone, and we were still at Serena's. After we slept it off, I said no more crack. I was ready to go.

Rowan looked at me, crestfallen. "No more crack? Our trip will be boring if we don't smoke crack."

Again, I gave in, but at last, we were on our way to South Padre Island. We took turns driving, smoking crack to stay awake, only stopping to pump gas or to use the bathroom. It felt so good to be out of Michigan. In Texas, we got a shitty hotel room for the night, and the next morning we drove around looking for the spring breakers. But there were none. It was just a sleepy little town. It was weird.

We drove to the ocean. I'd never seen it before, and it looked massive. I loved the sounds of the crashing waves and the chirping of ducks and birds hanging out by the shore. I felt happy, peaceful, and free. We asked one of the locals where the spring break parties were.

He said, "Kids, I'm sorry to tell you, but you're at the wrong place. This is North Padre Island, and South Padre Island is over three hours away."

Frustrated, we drove around Corpus Christi looking for drugs with no luck. On our way back to the motel, we pulled into a gas station to fill up, and as we drove away, a young woman using a payphone waved at us.

"No way," Rowan said. "I think we just got lucky." He turned the car around.

"What are you doing?" I asked.

"That woman's waving at us. She probably has drugs."

"Holy Moly, she is hot!" He stopped the car and backed up. "Let's bring her back to the motel and have sex with her."

Looking past him out the window, I fought back tears. I still liked Rowan. The first few nights of our vacation, I tried to coax him into having sex, but he refused, insisting it would be too weird because we were just friends.

Rowan waited until the hot woman was off the phone, asked if she needed a ride, and said she could spend the night with us if she hooked us up with drugs. She said she could get whatever we wanted. Rowan and I hadn't even had sex on our spring break vacation, and now he was picking up this random woman. I couldn't believe Rowan chose her over me.

We bought crack from her people and went back to our motel, but I didn't enjoy it because they were having sex in the bathroom while I watched TV by myself. But I was too high to feel much more than a vague sense of boredom and disappointment.

We drove to South Padre Island the next day and found the spring break party. There were young, beautiful people everywhere, and they all seemed so happy. We hung out on the beach and checked out the local strip club, where Rowan asked one of the dancers where we could find coke. She said she didn't know but recommended we try a smoke shop that had fake marijuana and cocaine and a lot of other silly stuff. We did and bought a little bit of each, but we didn't get high. It was getting late, so we decided to drive to Houston for the night and do the whippets we bought at the smoke shop. We took turns inhaling them in case Rowan passed out while driving, then I could take the steering wheel. We laughed and had a great time until we noticed the orange cones on the road. Rowan asked which way he should go, and I told him I had no idea. I had just inhaled nitrous oxide from a balloon, which made me feel like I was floating on clouds. I had no clue what was going on. He started following the cones toward the exit, and I got paranoid because I could see police cars just off the freeway. "Don't get off the freeway!" I yelled.

"What? Are you sure?"

"I'm pretty sure we don't have to stop. That exit is for big trucks only."

"I think you're wrong," he said, "but okay."

Rowan stayed on the freeway, and as soon as we passed the exit, he yelled, "Oh my God, we are so screwed!" I looked in the mirror and saw three police cars chasing after us, lights flashing.

The officers approached with guns drawn and yelled for us to step out of the car. They wanted to know why we didn't stop at the border checkpoint. We stayed silent.

"Where are the drugs?" Two officers interrogated us while others searched our car. They didn't find anything except empty whippet cartridges. We had to go back to the station so the K-9s could help them search for whatever they thought we were hiding. We followed one cop in his SUV as another drove beside us, and a third followed behind us back to the station. We wondered what the border cops would do with us.

"I can't believe you got us into such a big mess," Rowan yelled. "I'll be so screwed if I go to jail and my family finds out."

I tried to comfort him. "You're not going to jail because we don't have anything illegal with us."

When we got to the station, more officers and K-9s were waiting. My hands trembled as they told us to exit the car again and put us in handcuffs. Then they had the K-9s go through our car. They didn't find anything, except one officer found what he thought was weed. He grinned, holding up the bag of fake weed from the smoke shop. "I knew you guys were hiding something."

"It's not real," I said quickly. "Try it."

"It looks real to me." He tested it and discovered it was fake, and I almost felt bad for the guy. He really wanted to bust us. Another officer said, "Obviously, these kids are telling the truth. We made a mistake." He handed Rowan his driver's license. "Sir, you need to pay attention to the road." Then he took off our handcuffs and released us.

The following morning, we both felt rested and ready for our next adventure. In Houston, we began by visiting museums and going out to dinner. We were finally on a real vacation. But then we decided to find drugs. We crossed over into the rougher part of the city, and Rowan rolled down the window when we passed two scantily dressed women standing on the sidewalk. "Hey, do you ladies need a ride?"

They said sure and hopped in the car. Rowan didn't waste time, asking if they could hook us up. They took us to a dealer's house, where we hung out with them for a few more days before heading back to Michigan. By the time we got home, I was exhausted. It felt like we'd been gone forever.

Rowan's sister suspected he was doing drugs and blamed me for his addiction. I only met her a few times, but she told me to stay away from him or she'd call the cops. I wondered why she was so angry with me. After all, he was an adult and made his own decisions. Whenever Rowan's sister and mom showed up at his house, he asked me to hide under his bed until they left. One morning, Rowan and I were upstairs in his bed when we heard them walk through the front door. Freaking out, I bolted out of bed and pulled my clothes on.

"What's wrong?" Rowan asked. "Just get under the bed."

"My shoes are downstairs by the front door!"

"Okay, calm down," he said. "Get under the bed. I'll go talk to them."

He went downstairs, and his mom and sister began yelling. "Where is she? We know she's here because we found her shoes!"

From under the bed, I cringed, listening to every word. Rowan said I wasn't there and asked them to stop yelling. Ignoring him, Rowan's sister thumped up the stairs. "I bet she's hiding under his bed!" I held my breath as I watched her shoes walking towards me. "I know you're under there," she said. "You might as well come out or I'll drag you out by your hair."

My heart pounded as I realized there was no escape. She lifted the bed skirt and glared down at me. "You're busted." I crawled out, not knowing what else to do. She grabbed my arm. "Let's go."

Pulling away, I begged, "Don't touch me! I'll leave on my own."

"I should call the cops!"

"Go ahead," I said. "There are no drugs in the house." I rushed to the front door even though I had no idea where I was going.

"Wait up," Rowan said. "If you have to go, I'll take you to a friend's house."

His mom and sister begged him not to go, convinced we'd get more drugs. Rowan and I got in his truck and drove to Serena's. "Oh no," she exclaimed. "Bonnie and Clyde are back. I thought you forgot about me."

We told her what had happened and that we didn't have enough money to get a hotel room. "Can we hang out with you for the day?"

"Sure," she said, "As long as you have the money to get high."

For a while, we were smoking so much crack that a drug dealer was living on my sofa. Demetrius smoked weed and slept. We only woke him up when we ran out of drugs, and he'd take my car and drive out to Grand Rapids for more.

In late spring of 2002, a huge snowstorm blew through Muskegon and Grand Rapids. Demetrius got stuck in Grand Rapids for a few days because the roads were icy, then called to report that my car slid off the road into a ditch. He was okay but had to flee on foot through a field, leaving my car and the drugs behind. By the time Rowan and I got to Grand Rapids, my car had already been towed. I called the local towing company to see if they had my car. They told me they didn't, and suggested I call the cops, who'd tell me where it was.

Rowan insisted I had to tell the cops I was driving the car and lost control of it. We couldn't tell them Demetrius was driving my car because there was a warrant out for his arrest. I was nervous, and I realized I didn't have many options. When I called, the police wanted to know who was driving and why that person left the scene of an accident. I told them I was driving and had lost control of the car. "It was cold, so

I had my friend come pick me up," I lied.

They didn't believe me, insisting they saw a man's boot tracks in the snow leading away from the car. I stuck to my story and told them I was wearing big snow boots, but they kept asking who I was protecting and why. The impound company wasn't allowed to release the car until I made a statement to the police and signed it, but I was afraid they'd find out I was a crackhead and dismiss my story. Finally, Rowan said he had an awesome idea. We should scope out the impound lot at night and steal the car back.

That night, we went to the lot where we could see my car parked outside near a locked gate. All we needed was bolt cutters. We stood outside the fence discussing our plan when three big dogs charged toward us, barking. I ran back to Rowan's truck and told him there was no way we'd ever be able to get the car with those dogs guarding the place. He laughed and said all I had to do was distract the dogs with food while he cut the lock and drove my car away. I decided it was too dangerous and made him take me home.

More than a week had passed, and I wondered if it was even worth trying to get my car back. Then I remembered Demetrius had left the crack in the trunk. I called the officer back and made an appointment to go to the police station the next day. I was nervous, but I wanted my car back. And the crack.

I trembled as I talked to the officer, but it wasn't a big deal. Even so, I was so relieved when I drove the car away from the impound lot. When I got to my place, Rowan looked in the trunk where Demetrius claimed he'd stashed the crack. We couldn't believe it was still there. Score! We were so happy.

I started hanging out with Niko again, who kept us supplied with drugs and said he could get a lot more if he introduced me to a big-time dealer.

"You gotta have sex with him, and he'll give you crack in return," Niko explained. "Otherwise, we are literally fucked today."

I recoiled in horror at his suggestion. "No way! You've lost your mind, Niko. I don't know him. What if he hurts me?"

"Nothing's gonna happen to you," he promised.

Shaking my head, I was determined to stand my ground. "I haven't slept in almost thirty-six hours. I look like hell, and I don't have enough energy to have sex."

"Don't worry," Niko casually reassured me. "He doesn't care what you look like."

I slumped down into the couch. "Why is it my responsibility to get more drugs?"

Niko laughed. "Because you're the only hot blonde with a vagina, and that's the only way we'll get more crack today."

Rowan looked up from his crack pipe. "Naomi, you got this. Take one for the team."

I stared back at them, disgusted.

Rowan stood over me, waving the empty crack pipe. "I'll go with Niko to drop you off, so I know where you are."

I had so many questions sprinting through my head. What if this guy was disgusting? What would he think of me? Was I hot enough for him? Maybe it really didn't matter how I looked.

I finally agreed to do it. Niko called his dealer, Damien, and told him he had a hot blonde to meet. Then he told me to hurry up, take a shower, and get cleaned up because "Damien is ready for you." I felt like a piece of meat, but I felt better after taking a shower. At least we'd have crack for a while and the thought of getting high overshadowed any anxiety over the price I'd agreed to pay.

I told Rowan and Niko I was ready. They both smiled. "Don't worry," Rowan said. "We got your back, girl."

We pulled up to the house and Niko promised they'd be back in an hour. "Don't worry," he said. "Damien is a good guy."

I wondered how good of a guy he could be. He was a big-time drug dealer and about to exchange crack for sex. Niko walked me to the door. I felt like running away and screaming, but I didn't. Damien opened the door and Niko introduced us.

Damien invited me inside, and Niko and Rowan left. Damien could tell I was uncomfortable. "Don't be nervous," he said. "Make yourself at home." He was short and thin with a cute face, and his voice was soft and polite. I wondered how he could be so calm.

"You look beautiful today," he said. "I love your sexy red heels and your tight skirt."

"Thank you," I said. He seemed nice and I started to relax.

He led me to the couch, sat next to me, and leaned over and kissed me. His tongue was warm and gentle. I arched my back, raising my pelvis to his as his kiss grew probing and more intense. He pulled away and unhooked my bra, making my nipples tingle. I reached down and opened his belt buckle. His cock was hard and ready to escape. When it sprang from his boxers, he slid my red lace panties down to my ankles, crawled on top, and entered me. I put my hands on his hips to guide him. "Like this," I moaned. He propped himself up on one arm and slung one of my legs over his shoulder. The muscles in his arms flexed each time he thrust into me, and I grabbed onto them as I matched his rhythm. I got ready to climax. Too quickly, Damien yelled out, "I'm gonna cum!"

As he did, he pushed himself into me and cried out in relief. Then he rolled over and pulled me into his arms.

He sighed. "I'm sorry I came so fast."

"It's ok, I'm happy,' I assured him.

It wasn't so bad. I didn't have an orgasm, but it didn't last long, either. It could've been worse.

Damien gave me a big chunk of crack, and I felt good about taking one for the team. I knew Rowan and Niko would be happy.

Niko's first question as we drove away was, "Did you get the crack?" I pulled it out of my purse and their faces lit up. Niko chuckled. "Dang! He must really like blondes."

I laughed, too. "Maybe it's because I'm good in bed."

I had sex with Damien many times after that, and I also had sex with some other big-time drug dealers. They were my favorite: easy, quick, and no drama. And they always hooked me up with a fat crack rock before I left.

# CHAPTER EIGHT

For days at a time, all Rowan, Niko, and I did was obsessively play gin rummy and smoke crack. It became the never-ending story of my life. I was so sick of playing cards, yet we continued day after day. I wanted to pull my hair out in frustration, and sometimes I considered shaving my head. It didn't matter that I never wanted to play cards again. As soon as we bought more crack and I took that first hit, I was ready to play cards again.

Crack suppressed my appetite, so I wasn't eating much. I went from 115 to 95 pounds in four months. Then Rowan and I came home one night to find an eviction notice on my door, and the utilities shut off. I wondered what I would do with all the beautiful furniture and the big TV that Dan had given me.

"Don't worry," Rowan said. "We'll sell your TV and furniture."

We gathered some of my belongings, but there wasn't enough room in Rowan's little truck to take everything. Besides, we didn't have a new place to put it.

A few weeks later, we went to get the rest of my stuff and found another notice on the door. Anything left in the apartment would be confiscated until I paid the money I owed. I wanted to cry because I worked hard to get my apartment, and I was devastated to lose it. I began gathering everything important to me when I noticed Rowan peeping out the blinds. "We have to get out of here right now," he whispered.

"We need to get my stuff first," I argued, trying to cram everything I could into a garbage bag.

Rowan was freaking out. "No way. There's no time. They're here."

"Who's here?" I tried to look out the window, but he shooed me away.

"Undercover cops. We gotta go out the back door."

Ignoring his panic, I continued packing. "You're paranoid."

Rowan turned pale. "We can never come back here again, and I'm leaving with or without you."

Pushing him out of the way, I looked out the window and saw nothing unusual. "You're losing your mind."

"Let's go!" he insisted.

His paranoia got to me, and I grabbed a few more things and ran out the back door after him. I was infuriated, knowing I'd never be able to get the rest of my belongings. Some things were important to me, like the prayer books my parents had given me, my GED, my birth certificate, and my Amish report cards.

I was no longer working or going to college. All I wanted to do was smoke crack. The need for it consumed me. When I had the money, I stayed in motel rooms but sometimes, I slept on floors or couches with random crackheads. Once completely broke, I called Dan for help, and he insisted on meeting for breakfast.

He watched me scarf down my food as if I hadn't eaten in days, which I hadn't. He sighed and shook his head. "You need to stop hanging out with these bad people, Naomi. I want you to come home with me. I'll take care of you until you're back on your feet."

I shook my head. Deep down, I knew I needed help, but I kept telling myself I was fine, and that Dan was just a dirty old man trying to keep me from hanging out with my friends. He begged me to let him help, so I told him he could buy me a new tire for my car and give me some money so I could eat. He gave me some cash, and I told him I appreciated his kindness.

I left Dan at the diner, feeling hopeless and alone. I no longer cared about anyone or anything, including myself. I'd lost touch with myself and everything I was taught. As the days turned into weeks and weeks into months, I fell deeper and deeper into a lifeless crack pit. No matter how awful it got and how wrong I knew it was, I couldn't gather enough strength to stop. When Niko told me he needed my help making money, I agreed, as long as I didn't have to steal anything. He said no stealing. "All you have to do is have sex."

I was so addicted that I didn't care anymore and told him he could count on me, figuring it would only be for a little while. Undoubtedly, I'd be strong enough to stop smoking crack soon. Niko called his buddy to tell him he had a hot blonde looking for some fun. His friend got super excited. "Great," I thought, "more madness."

When we showed up, there were two guys instead of one, but they ended up being pretty cool, and I saw them every week for a few months. Niko kept introducing me to more guys to support our growing crack habit. Most of them were more strung out than I was. I became numb and felt I had no choice. I wished I could go back in time and choose a different path. But I only cared about crack.

It seemed almost every day, wherever I was, the cops showed up for one reason or another. I was so ashamed of who I'd become—a prostitute to support my crack habit. How could I let this happen when I'd grown up in such a protective, sheltered environment?

The unruly and unpredictable river my parents warned me about had finally consumed me, and I was drowning. It had been over a year since I'd visited my family. They wrote to me, but I never wrote back. My youngest sister later told me they often prayed I was still alive.

In 2003, Niko introduced me to Amir, a businessman who owned several gas stations, and offered to let me stay with him for a while. In return, Amir requested that I dress to impress his many friends who came over to get laid. I took them to the bedroom one by one. Amir didn't allow me to ask them for money, but they usually left me ten or twenty dollars. I felt abused and disgusted with myself and wanted to run away, but I had nowhere to go.

Having sex with all those men wasn't a pleasant experience. I lay there pretending I was somewhere else, anywhere else, then tried to erase it from my memory. I hated living with Amir, but my other options were to sleep under a bridge or stay with random crackheads or at the crack house. That crack house was scary because addicts went there when they had no other place to go. It didn't have running water, and it was filthy. Serena once took me there to buy crack when our other dealers weren't available. At least with Amir, I had a roof over my head, and he was an excellent cook, so I always had food to eat.

Once a week, Rowan picked me up so we could hang out and get high with the money I made. When it was gone, I went back to Amir's. I craved a normal life, but I became convinced that wasn't possible.

Amir announced that my life was about to change. I'd been awake smoking crack for two days and couldn't wait to hear about it. Maybe he had a way for me to escape this horrible nightmare. Amir said his friend wanted to buy a blonde American girl for ten thousand dollars to be his wife in Iraq. I asked if I'd have to go to Iraq by myself or if I could bring a friend. Would I have to be there forever? Was it safe?

Amir said I'd go alone and stay for at least two years unless my husband wanted kids and then I'd have to stay indefinitely. He said going to Iraq was a chance to start over and have a good life, a chance to get away from crack.

I'd never heard of such a crazy offer. "This guy must be hideous if he has to buy a wife. Why can't he find a wife like other people?" I asked.

Amir shrugged and said I could sleep on it. He had a few other girls that were interested if I wasn't. I told Rowan about Amir's offer, and Rowan said ten grand wasn't nearly enough and I should ask for one hundred thousand dollars. I called Amir back to tell him I'd marry his friend for one hundred thousand dollars. "You've lost your mind!" Amir yelled. "Do you think you're a member of the Royal family or something?"

The more I thought about it, the more I realized it was a bad idea. I said no to Amir's offer. I had zero motivation to do anything other than to get high. Occasionally, I checked in with Dan so he wouldn't worry too much. He took me to eat and told me how skinny I was. "I know you're doing drugs," he said. I denied his accusation. Sometimes he had tears in his eyes, which made me feel worse.

That summer, I decided I had to get away from Amir, and the only way to do that was to go back to work. I found a strip club in Grand Rapids called The Red Barn. The girls didn't seem to like me, but I didn't care. I wasn't there to impress them. I was there solely to make money so Rowan and I would have a place to sleep, food to eat, and, most importantly, crack. Most nights, we stayed at the Ramada Inn down the road from the club. Rowan dropped me off at work and I'd make three to seven hundred dollars for an eight-hour shift.

All the girls at The Red Barn had problems. Most were addicted to drugs like I was. Others had abusive boyfriends, and some were just down and out. They smoked crack and meth in the bathroom and snorted cocaine in the dressing room. We were all messed up in one way or another. It was a very uncomfortable work environment. I tried to ignore the girls as much as possible, but some drama was unavoidable. I never smoked crack at work because I was focused on making money.

Later that summer, Rowan's uncle asked us to demolish an old, empty house on ten acres he owned in Howard City, thirty minutes outside the city. We spent weekends tearing it down one section at a time. We built a bonfire in the backyard, smoked crack, and went for walks in the woods. We hunted woodchucks, quails, and pheasants. Then we cleaned, prepared, and cooked them on the fire. A few months later, we moved a trailer onto the new property. There was no electricity or heat, but I was happy because we finally had a safe place to stay.

Little by little, I started letting Dan into my life again. I didn't have many options. By this time, Rowan and I were staying in the trailer full-time, and Dan brought us food. He knew we were doing drugs but didn't say anything. I think he was just happy to know where I was. One night, he showed up with a big bucket of fried chicken and several side orders. I was just about to take a drag from the crack pipe. Stuffing the pipe under a cushion, I jumped up, yelling at Dan for coming by unannounced. He said he was worried and figured we were hungry.

"I didn't ask you to come by," I snapped. I wasn't thinking clearly because I hadn't slept or eaten anything in two days.

After dinner, I retrieved the pipe and walked down to the river to get high. In my paranoia, I kept thinking I heard footsteps behind me. I was so afraid Dan would come looking for me and see me smoking. After I returned, I hid the pipe in the trailer, apologized to Dan, and thanked him for bringing food.

"You're not yourself when you're high," Dan said in his quiet way.

He looked into the fire. "Rowan and I talked while you were gone, and he told me."

I glared at Rowan in disbelief.

Rowan shrugged. "Sorry, but I don't know what else to do because this is getting worse. Maybe Dan can help us."

I put my head in my hands, trying not to cry.

"It's okay, Naomi," Dan assured me. "I'm not mad. I knew the whole time, and I want to help you. I cry at night just thinking about it and knowing you need help, but I don't want to scare you away."

"Let's all get high!" Rowan shouted.

"No way," I said. "Dan can't smoke crack because he has a bad heart."

Dan laughed. "Sure, I can. We only live once. And if that's the only way I get to hang out with you, then you can bet your ass we're all getting high tonight."

I stood up. "I don't think you should, Dan. What if you have a heart attack?"

"I'll be fine. If it kills me, oh well. At least I went out with a bang."

He was determined so I stopped arguing with him. Rowan was right. We were all adults. Dan took his first drag and started coughing. "Do you feel anything?" I asked.

"Not much," he answered.

"You should be high because you took a huge hit."

He looked up at me. "What am I supposed to feel?"

Rowan and I grinned. "High as the clouds."

Suddenly, Dan jumped up from the couch, ecstatic. "Let's do something!"

We played cards and smoked until we ran out of crack.

Dan was an engineer, but after he started smoking crack, he missed work and got into trouble with his boss. Rowan kept telling Dan he should retire before he got fired and lost his quarter of a million-dollar pension. When Dan came to the trailer to announce that he'd officially retired, Rowan and I joined in his excitement.

Dan's retirement was the beginning of the end. I quit working at the Red Barn, and we drained his savings account, then waited for his pension to cash out. When the money transfer went through, we went bonkers. The dealer brought out a huge rock of crack that looked like a block of homemade Amish soap. I was so excited to bring home an ounce of rock. This meant we could smoke for a long time. Then we left, got a hotel room, and smoked and played cards for three days.

The twenty thousand dollars Dan transferred lasted barely a month. Dan didn't say much about it, but I knew he was upset. Even so, he called the bank to transfer another ten thousand dollars. When he hung up, he said, "We need to watch our spending habits." We were facing another week without any money.

We survived by eating at restaurants and pumping gas, then taking off without paying. Rowan called it dine-n-dash and gas-n-go. We also went out into the woods at dusk one evening and shot a deer. I didn't think it could get much worse and had no idea how to climb out of this hole. Smoking crack ruined my ability to see a way out. We stayed awake smoking crack for days. Rowan kept trying to make me eat, but I refused.

At the end of the fifth day, I was so delirious and weak that I felt like I might collapse. I went to the bathroom. I saw the toilet filling up with blood. I thought I was dying. I called for Rowan and Dan to help me, but they didn't respond. A gloom I'd never felt before enveloped my body. I felt like I was dragging myself down the hallway, begging them to help me. They were right there, sitting at the dining room table, waiting for me to return. I yelled their names, but they wouldn't look at me. They continued their conversation as if I wasn't there. I felt myself slipping away. My life flashed before my eyes, and I could see my mom and dad and the siblings I'd left behind. Their faces looked so sad, like shattered mirrors, melting and dripping. I could see how much I hurt them when I left. And I realized how much I missed them. Suddenly, I wanted to live.

I called out Dan's name again. This time, he came running. He found me on the floor, blood everywhere, which turned out to be from my period. Crying, Dan picked me up and carried me to the bed. Falling in and out of consciousness, I assured him I was dying. With tears rolling down his cheeks, Dan said, "No way, it's not your time to go. Hold on and stay awake."

"It's too hard," I whispered, my voice growing weaker. Dan begged me to try harder as I felt my soul trying to leave my body. "I'm scared, Dan," I gasped. "Something keeps pulling me away." I was struggling for my life.

Dan told Rowan to go to the store for juice and food. After he returned, Dan forced me to drink, and I started feeling a little better. Dan looked confused when I asked why he didn't help me sooner. "I came running as soon as you called my name," he said.

My hands trembled, and my hair was damp with sweat. I shook my head. "I came out to the dining room. I was calling out to both of you. I was right there, and you just ignored me."

Rowan and Dan both insisted I never came out of the bathroom.

I was afraid to fall asleep, worried I might not wake up. Dan said I wasn't allowed to smoke crack anymore, and I assured him I never wanted to smoke again. He told Rowan to flush the rest down the toilet, but Rowan refused. He wasn't the one on his deathbed, he said.

Finally, I fell asleep. When I woke several hours later, they were still playing cards and smoking. Rowan jokingly asked if I wanted to hit the pipe, and I laughed, even though I didn't think it was funny.

# CHAPTER NINE

After three days of sleep and some food, I began to reflect on my life. I'd escaped death and needed to make major changes if I wanted to continue my journey on earth. I wondered why I couldn't stop being self-destructive. Why did I continue to live in such misery? I couldn't understand how I got so weak that I allowed a drug to destroy me. A few years ago, I felt so mentally strong. It was time to figure out what kept me from changing my life. I cried like a baby because I felt so lost. Surely, I'd hit rock bottom.

Dan and I sat on the couch, away from Rowan and the crack smoke. He awkwardly put his arm around my shoulder, reassuring me that everything would be okay. He told me not to give up, and that I needed to be stronger than ever. I had no strength left at all, but his words felt empowering. "You have to look deep inside yourself and find what you want out of life," Dan said.

I kept telling him there was no hope for me unless I quit drugs.

"Do you really mean that, Naomi?" Dan asked. "Because you've told me that many times."

"I always mean it," I replied, "but something takes over, and I smoke again no matter how much I don't want to." I told Dan and Rowan we needed to change our routine and maybe do some hiking and other outdoor activities. "We need a real home," I told them.

Determined to stop living in hell, I found an apartment in Plainfield and saw a tiny glimmer of hope again. We decided to have one more blowout before moving in and promised each other this would be the last time. The new apartment was off-limits. We even did a pinky swear.

The apartment had a balcony where I could sit and watch birds feast at the feeders in the yard. At night, deer grazed in the backyard. It was a peaceful place to live. Rowan took the smaller bedroom, and Dan and I took the master. I wasn't thrilled about my lack of privacy but didn't make a big deal out of it. At first, I slept in the bed with Dan, separated by a rolled-up blanket wedged between us. He didn't like the partition, but Dan had hygiene issues. I couldn't handle it. Eventually, I moved to the couch. Dan was offended that I didn't want to sleep in his bed anymore.

The three of us quickly got on each other's nerves. We went sightseeing and hiking to keep our minds occupied. I thought about getting a job dancing again, but I was unmotivated. Rowan also considered returning to work because Dan's retirement money was running out. We'd smoked nearly a quarter of a million dollars in less than six months — what a waste.

We went on yet another bender, and I was more depressed than ever. It felt like my life was over because we were smoking crack in the apartment, which I swore I'd never do. Moving into a new apartment was supposed to give me a fresh start, but mentally, I still wasn't strong enough to say no to crack. Not knowing what to do or where to turn, I began to feel suicidal. I was hopeless, and I had no one to blame but myself. I wanted to run away and even thought about being Amish again. I missed my family. My sadness drifted away as I remembered the good times I had growing up. Maybe it was my destiny to be Amish. Was that the only way I'd be able to stop smoking crack? Was that the only way that I'd ever find peace again? For a moment, I wanted to leave everything behind for a new life with my Amish family.

Sitting on my bedroom floor, I looked through a black duffle bag where I kept my most precious memories. Inside, I found the Amish singing book my dad gave me when I joined The Singing. I pulled it out, tracing the worn leather with my finger and remembering the pride in my dad's eyes when he handed it to me. I also found some Amish trinkets and toys from my childhood, the green wallet I had in my pocket when I ran away, and a book of important addresses and phone numbers. The little book meant so much to me when I was Amish that I took it with me.

As I flipped through the pages, a square of paper slipped out and floated to the floor. I picked it up and unfolded it, recognizing the name and number. Earlier in my addiction, Niko offered to introduce me to a "nice older man" named Randy with whom I could make easy money. At first, I wasn't interested but Rowan and Niko insisted, reminding me I could save the day by having a little sex. As usual, I agreed, and they drove me to meet him.

Randy was a gentleman, a tall, heavyset bald man in his sixties who smelled of cigarettes, and he walked with hunched shoulders and a slight limp. He only wanted to give me oral sex, which I enjoyed, so we got straight to business. I quickly faked an orgasm and made a hundred dollars in less than fifteen minutes.

Until then, I'd forgotten about Randy. I called him right away. Randy asked what was new and I told him what was going on, trying not to overwhelm him with details. I was too embarrassed to tell him everything. Randy said he was going to Las Vegas and invited me to go with him. I replied that I was touched but had to decline because I didn't have the money for a plane ticket. Randy laughed and said he'd take care of it. My heart skipped a beat. I couldn't believe it. I'd never flown anywhere or been to Las Vegas. I was beyond excited.

I told Dan and Rowan I was going to Las Vegas, California. They looked confused and asked if I was going to Las Vegas or California, and I assured them I was going to Las Vegas, California. Laughing, they told me Las Vegas was in Nevada, not California. I felt dumb. In school, I only learned about states, not cities. Part of me hoped I'd find a happy new life in Las Vegas. At the same time, I knew I had to live life one day at a time while making some big changes. I didn't understand why Randy was being so kind to me. He owed me nothing, but I decided to be grateful.

Rowan and Dan dropped me off at the airport. I'd never been inside an airport before, and I was nervous. The terminal was crowded with people waiting in lines and rushing to get somewhere, and I wondered how I'd find my way to the plane in time. Breathing deeply, I tried to stay calm. When I got my ticket and went through security, a nice lady directed me to the gate where Randy was having coffee and reading the paper. I wondered how he could be so relaxed knowing we were about to get on a plane. He greeted me but didn't say much. I felt uneasy.

"Is everything okay?" I asked.

"Yes," he answered. "Just reading the morning paper, as usual. Must I remind you I'm a man of few words?"

Right, I remembered. Randy had described himself as anti-social. Feeling a bit more relaxed, I smiled. "I remember now."

We boarded the plane and Randy offered me the window seat since it was my first time. My anxiety turned into excitement, and I was surprised by how big the plane was inside. Randy raised the window shade so I could watch the city slip away as we rose higher and higher. My ears got clogged, which Randy explained was normal. He gave me a piece of gum to help pop them back open. I soon realized flying wasn't a big deal and fell asleep.

I woke up just as the pilot announced we were passing over the Hoover Dam and looked out the window. The dam curled through the brown landscape below, then disappeared into the desert. We emerged over the snow-peaked mountains and there was the city of Las Vegas. How exciting!

Outside, I was shocked by how many casinos there were and wondered why any place would need so much of the same thing. Yet it was so glamorous, and we'd only traveled a short distance. Randy said this was just the beginning. "Wait until dark because it looks different with all the lights on." For the first time in ages, I felt alive.

After settling in at his spacious apartment, Randy asked what I wanted to do first. I admitted I had no idea. I didn't know a thing about Vegas. Randy suggested we go downtown to the Golden Nugget because he wanted to put in his bets. I wasn't sure what he meant, but I soon discovered he was betting on sports. We headed straight for the bar where Randy put money into a machine. The bartender served him a drink and then walked away without expecting payment. Confused, I decided to sit back and observe and quickly learned why gamblers were drinking for free. Randy asked if I wanted to play, and I reminded him I didn't have any money. He just smiled and told me to stop worrying about money. "Go have fun," he said, slipping forty dollars into my hand. "Just be careful, stay alert, and check in with me once in a while." I promised I would and went off to play the slots.

Before I knew it, the money was gone, and I returned to Randy. "What happened?" he asked.

"I lost it all."

He chuckled and took my hand, leading me out of the casino. "Let me make it up to you."

Back at his apartment, Randy held up a one-hundred-dollar bill, ripped it in half, handed me one half, and said I could have the other half after I allowed him to give me a real orgasm. I stared at the torn money, speechless for a moment. How did he know I'd faked my orgasm the first time we met? Amused and turned on, I got undressed and flopped back on the couch, legs spread and eyes closed. He knelt in front of me, massaged my breasts, then moved down my body, caressing my thighs before slipping a finger inside me. My back arched, and my hips raised to meet his warm tongue. He hungrily ate me, tracing figure eights on my aroused clit. I moaned.

"Just like that! I'm so close," I whispered. I grabbed his head. "I'm gonna cum!" Then I breathed a sigh of relief and just lay there, relaxed. Could this be real? Was I really in Las Vegas with this generous man?

When I opened my eyes, Randy stood over me with the bill taped together. "Jackpot," he said.

Randy advised me to go back to the casino and play the penny machines to make his money last longer. After a while, I got the hang of it and won a little money.

Later that week, Randy took me to the main strip to buy clothes and eat at amazing restaurants. We saw the Bellagio fountains, the Atlantis show at Caesars Palace, and the Star Trek experience at the Hilton. He even set up a helicopter tour over the Grand Canyon and sent another woman along so I wouldn't be alone. Nervous, I asked if he could please go with us, but he just laughed and reminded me he was scared of heights and wouldn't be caught dead on a helicopter.

Even with all the activity, Randy worried that I was bored, but I assured him I was having the time of my life. What a life-changing adventure! I couldn't believe such a place existed. It blew my mind, and I'd only been there for a short time. Randy was a complete gentleman the entire time. Occasionally, he gave me oral sex, insisting that he enjoyed making me happy. We never had intercourse.

We were gambling in a little bar when Randy suggested I check out the Stratosphere. I asked if he was coming.

"No way," he repeated. "It's too high for my taste."

I shook my head. "Then no. I'd be too scared by myself."

"Maybe you need to go alone to build your confidence again."

He was right. I had no confidence left after being a crackhead for two years. The next day, Randy dropped me off at the Stratosphere Casino & Hotel and told me to have fun. My heart pounded as I strolled through the massive building, trying to figure out how to get to the top. I finally had to ask a security guard for help.

Once I got up there, I could see most of Vegas, which was a thrill. I'd never seen anything like it. Then I went on all the incredible rides. When I came back downstairs, I gambled my leftover money and ended up winning two hundred-fifty dollars. I felt so positive and confident, and I couldn't wait to tell Randy how much fun I had going on such an adventure by myself.

His face lit up when he saw me. "You look like you enjoyed your afternoon. Are you ready to go home yet?"

Five days had passed with two left to go. The thought of going home filled me with disappointment. I wasn't ready to go back to Michigan because I finally felt like a human being again. Randy saw the sadness on my face.

This is the one room schoolhouse I attended.

This is the farm we moved to when I was 12. The 2nd set of buildings
on the right is the farm we moved from. The picture was taken from
the top of the silo, which was attached to the barn.

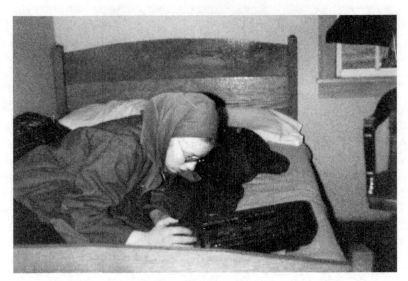

This is one of the first pictures of me. I was 15 and
on my bed with my battery powered radio.

I was 16 and still Amish trying on my
English clothes I bought at a yardsale.

My white horse, Prince, and I got second place at a horse show.

This is the first picture of me after I left the Amish. I was wearing the short black shorts Christina bought for me at Walmart. I didn't know how to ride a bicycle, so I rode this tricycle instead.

Me in the buggy on my way to town with
my brother after I left the Amish.

Amish women always wear a bonnet over their *kapp*
when they go away. Here I was in town.

Dancing at a Christmas party 2012.
*Photo by Steve Chelski*

Dancing at a Christmas party 2012.
*Photo by Steve Chelski*

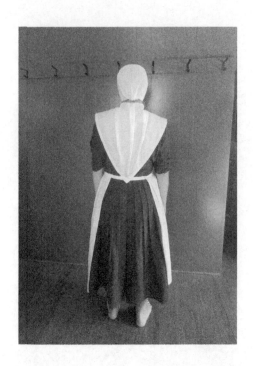

Two views of how I dressed for church.

Ready for church at my sister's house in 2018.

Visiting my parents for Christmas 2014.

Visiting my family 2015.

Ready to go on stage.

My first birthday cake and party when I turned 18.

My partner and I at a wedding.

"If you want, we can change our flights and stay another week," he offered.

I gasped. "Really? I'd love that!"

Randy shook his head. "I'm definitely spoiling you."

After jumping up and down, I hugged him. "I know, and it feels so good to be spoiled and sober."

I couldn't believe how often I won money playing the penny machines. By the end of the second week, I'd won almost three thousand dollars. Every day, Randy gave me his winning slips to take to the cashier because he didn't like to deal with people. He let me keep some money, claiming I'd earned it. I felt so lucky.

I fantasized about moving to Las Vegas, but I knew I couldn't maintain the lifestyle I'd gotten used to with Randy. He kept asking what my plan was once I got back to Michigan. I had no idea, but I promised to stay away from drugs, and I truly meant it. I had no intention of ever smoking again, but I didn't have a plan. The night before we went back to Michigan, Randy made me promise that I wouldn't give the money to Rowan and Dan to buy crack.

It was tough for me to get on the plane. I knew I couldn't live in a fantasy world forever, but I felt ready to take on whatever the real world threw at me. Even so, the more I thought about Rowan and Dan, the more I got that awful craving deep down in my stomach. Before the plane even landed, all I could think about was crack, but I kept telling myself I was stronger than ever and wouldn't let anyone or anything take that away again. The cravings grew as I waited for Rowan and Dan to pick me up.

Dan said I seemed like a different person, and he was happy for me. I told them my head was finally clear and I could think again. It was mid-January, and when we stepped outside, there was snow everywhere. The sun was bright, and everything glistened.

"Where are we going anyway?" Rowan asked as Dan drove away from the airport. I suggested we go for a hike because the weather was so refreshing. They agreed, but we couldn't decide on a place to go. I really didn't care. The air in Vegas felt thick and polluted, and I just wanted to be outside. I stuck my head out the window, breathing in the cool, fresh Michigan air. We began chatting and laughing, and I felt the crack cravings subside. That's when Rowan reminded me that I had more friends who'd missed me. I knew what he was thinking because he had that big ear-to-ear grin on his face. "Let me guess," I said. "Phil and Serena."

"You guessed it," he said. "We should go visit them."

I slumped down in the back seat, knowing what would happen if we did. I tried to stay strong and ignore the cravings, but I failed and finally gave in. I said, "Okay, as long as we don't smoke crack." Rowan and Dan agreed. We'd only visit with them for a little bit and wouldn't smoke.

Serena and her boyfriend, Phil, looked happy to see me. Serena pulled me aside and commented on how amazing I looked. I told her I felt amazing and never wanted to smoke crack again. She laughed and said, "Good luck."

"You need to stop hanging out with the crazies," she said. Meaning Rowan and Dan. "Otherwise, you'll never be able to stop. They're the reason you started smoking crack in the first place."

"No," I protested. "I'm the only one to blame for my habit. Rowan and Dan are my friends. I can't imagine not having them in my life. They're the only people always there for me no matter what."

The room fell silent. Rowan kept looking across the room at me, smiling, and I knew what he was thinking.

"Naomi!" he called out. "You're the one with all the money. Can we smoke crack for old times' sake?"

Serena looked at me with one eyebrow raised. "No way," I told him. "I promised Randy I'd never smoke crack again." The real reason was that I finally felt good and didn't want to be depressed again.

Just as Rowan seemed to be giving up, I gave the go-ahead. The cravings were stronger than my willpower. I called my dealer. What a mess — I was so depressed and mad at myself for giving in. At first, I was also angry with Rowan, but I realized it wasn't his fault. I wanted to smoke crack from the moment I got on the plane back to Michigan.

I had no one to blame but myself. How could I ever face Randy again? Not only did I break my promise to him, but I also broke my promise to myself.

The money I'd won in Vegas wouldn't last long. Soon I'd have to decide between getting a job or calling Randy. I wasn't well enough to work. I only hoped that Randy would be kind enough to take me to Vegas again. Rowan, Dan, and I continued smoking crack and burned through all the money. Every day, I wondered where I'd go and what I'd do when the money was gone. I thought Randy would judge me if I asked him to take me to Vegas again. But I felt desperate, so I called him and casually asked when he was going back to Vegas.

"What happened?" Randy asked. "Don't tell me you spent all that money already."

Embarrassed to admit the truth, I hesitated. "I'm depressed living in boring old Michigan when the most exciting city in the world is just a short plane ride away."

Randy laughed. "You were terrified to fly and now you can't wait to get back on the plane. Well, I'm going back the week after next, and you're welcome to come with me."

My heart filled with glee, but I tried to keep my cool. Being in Vegas was better than being on drugs. I had time to reflect on who I was and the path forward. I knew if I stayed in Michigan, I'd probably always be an addict. I was ready to make better choices for the sake of my future.

Two nights before my flight to Vegas, Rowan, Dan, and I decided to smoke crack "one last time." What was one more night? I could rest the second day, so I looked good when I met Randy on the plane. Instead, we smoked and played cards until it was time for them to drive me to the airport. We had no idea it snowed all night. When we got on the road, it was still falling hard and fast, icing over the streets and slowing us down. I lost hope of getting to Vegas, but for a moment, I felt relieved because I was too exhausted and embarrassed to see Randy.

When we arrived at the airport, my plane was already boarding, and I still had to get my boarding pass. "There's no way I'll make it in time," I cried.

In a stern voice, Dan grabbed my hand and said, "You are making it onto that plane. Run as fast as you can!" He tried to smile through the pained expression on his face. I gave him one last grateful look, then sped to the counter where the attendant said the door was about to close. She called the gate to let them know I was on my way, and I ran as fast as I could, dragging my luggage behind me.

Miraculously, I made it onto the plane, where a handsome flight attendant greeted me. "It's about time," he said, winking. "We were waiting for you. You almost missed your flight."

I was so out of breath I could barely walk. People stared as I stumbled down the aisle. It felt like forever, but I finally found Randy reading the newspaper. He just looked at me and shook his head. "Looks like someone had a long night."

I couldn't look him in the eye. "I don't feel good."

Randy had a cool attitude, like he'd been through a lot and was too old and wise for any nonsense. He showed no emotion, instead exuding calm confidence. I had the jitters and needed some nutrition, so I ordered an orange juice. When Randy handed it to me, I dropped it and spilled it all over my lap. I was too tired to care. I just wanted to sleep.

When we got to Randy's apartment in Vegas, I fell fast asleep. The next day I felt brand new again. We stayed in Vegas for two weeks, gambling, going to movies, trying different restaurants, and hanging out with his friends. Before I knew it, I had to go back to Michigan. Again, I was bringing home around three thousand dollars.

Randy watched as I counted my money. "Promise me you won't give that hard-earned money to those boys," he said.

"I promise I won't make that mistake again," I said. In my heart, I knew I wasn't strong enough and my words were hollow.

Sure enough, nothing changed. I went back to Vegas twice over the next few months, and each time I felt a surge of hope that I could turn things around in Michigan. Dan was living on disability and welfare because we'd spent all his retirement money on crack. Rowan was looking for a job, but I still had no ambition. We were all depressed.

Finally, I told Rowan and Dan I wanted to move to Vegas. Rowan laughed, and Dan banged his fist on the table. "You think running away from your problems will fix everything?"

Frustrated, I dropped my head into my hands. I guess he didn't want what was best for me after all. "I'm not trying to run away from my problems," I argued. "I want to start a new life and take care of myself again."

Dan took a deep breath. "I'm afraid for your safety," he said quietly.

"I appreciate it, but Randy would never let anything happen to me."

"Neither would I," Dan replied. He continued sulking.

Randy warned me that Vegas was too scary for a girl like me, but he wouldn't elaborate. I wondered what he meant, but I didn't ask because I didn't want to know. Eventually, Randy explained that everywhere you look in Vegas, there are drugs and dealers. He even drove me through all the depressed areas of the city one night so I could see how bad it was.

"You think living on the streets in Michigan is bad, think again."

I looked out his car window at a woman dragging herself down the street barefoot, high as a kite. Others were slumped over on the sidewalk. "What do you recommend I do then? I can't stay in Michigan. I'm so stuck and unhappy there."

"Maybe you should try rehab," he said.

"Ugh," I thought, "no way." When I was in Vegas, I never craved crack. It felt like an epiphany. I needed to get away from Michigan. Otherwise, I'd probably always be a crackhead. I told Randy I didn't need rehab. I only thought about smoking crack when I was with my so-called friends in Michigan. But Randy just shook his head. "I don't think it's a good idea."

I couldn't stop thinking about it, but I had no idea how to make it happen. Randy and I did everything we liked to do while in Vegas, and I fantasized about what my life would be like if I moved there. Would I be a dancer, a waiter, or a dealer at a casino? My imagination ran wild. I felt like I could be unstoppable.

One weekend, I went into a tourist shop to wait for Randy and look for postcards to send to my family. I stood there by the rack, trying to tell if they needed stamps. A handsome guy wearing dress pants and a tie stood nearby looking at the shot glasses, so I shyly asked him if I needed stamps to mail the postcards.

He looked surprised that I was talking to him. "I don't work here." His face broke into a sweet, crooked smile.

I could feel myself blushing. "I'm sorry," I said. "You look very professional."

His brown hair was parted on one side and slicked back with gel. He reminded me of Keanu Reeves, one of my favorite actors.

"Where are you from and why so many postcards?" he asked.

The butterflies fluttered in my stomach as we joked around. He said his name was Lance and gave me his number. "No pressure but call me if you get bored and want to go to dinner and a show while you're in town."

I bought the postcards and walked back to the Golden Nugget to meet Randy, wondering if I should tell him about meeting Lance or keep it to myself and sneak out. I felt torn because I wanted to make new friends, but I'd just met this guy in a store. What if he was a serial killer? But if I wanted to start over, I had to take some chances. So, I told Randy. He looked skeptical but nodded his head. "The guys here might seem nice, but they're only trying to get something from you. Be safe and take your time. Get to know him first."

I felt restless, not knowing if I should call Lance, worried that maybe I felt that way because no one had noticed or talked to me for a long time. Again, I asked Randy what I should do, and he said it wasn't up to him.

When I finally called Lance, we discovered that we had a lot in common. He noticed my accent and I told him I grew up Amish. Lance said that when he was a kid, his parents dropped him and his brother at an Amish farm while they went on vacation. What a small world. Talking to someone who seemed to have a normal, happy life was so refreshing. I wanted to talk to him forever. He invited me to go to dinner and a show the following night.

Lance took me on my first real date since I'd started doing drugs. He took me to a restaurant in the Stratosphere and a live cabaret show afterward. He did all the boyfriend things I'd been missing out on, like opening the door for me and holding my hand.

Over the next two weeks, I learned that Lance didn't exactly have the happy, normal life I'd first imagined. He'd gotten caught with over a hundred pounds of marijuana and spent a few years in prison. He still smoked a lot of weed, hitting the bong even when he got up to pee. But it didn't bother me. We were both trying to get our life on track, which made me feel closer to him.

I really wanted to stay. Lance listened to me talk about my situation in Michigan and how much I wanted to move to Vegas. He thought it was a great idea. All I had was the three thousand dollars I'd won at the penny machines, and I knew that wouldn't last long once I returned to Michigan and hung out with Rowan and Dan.

My hands trembled slightly as I asked Lance if I could move in with him.

His dark, sleepy eyes lit up. "Of course! I wouldn't want it any other way." I hugged him, surging with excitement.

In May, on my twenty-fourth birthday, I flew back to Michigan for the last time. This time was different because I'd decided to move to Las Vegas. Dan tried to convince me that I was making the wrong choice because Lance was a stranger. I told him he was being selfish and that I knew enough about Lance to know I'd be safe.

Randy said he was going back to Vegas eleven days later. I could hardly wait. Every day felt like a week. I had to slow down and cherish those last few days with Dan and Rowan because I didn't know when I'd see them again. They were the only people in my life who'd been there for me in the past two years, but I had to follow my heart. I didn't want to live another day like I'd lived for the past two years. I knew I would die if I kept smoking crack. Some days my heart felt like it could stop beating any moment from an overdose.

As I gathered the few belongings I had left from the apartment, I thought about everything I lost when I got evicted. I worked so hard to get my life together before the drugs and nearly destroyed it in such a short time. It was hard to reconcile. My daze suddenly lifted, and I felt relieved and free. It dawned on me that all the things I lost were material things holding me back. I'd survived a miserable trainwreck and felt grateful to be alive. The destructive path I was following would lead me out of the frying pan into the fire of Las Vegas, the city of sin.

# CHAPTER TEN

Moving day finally came. Saying goodbye to Dan and Rowan at the airport was hard. We all had tears in our eyes as they told me they loved me very much and to be careful. I promised I would and that I'd always love them, too. As I turned to walk away, tears streamed down my face. Then I remembered why I was moving and stopped crying. I started thinking about all the new adventures ahead.

When we got to Vegas, Randy took me to lunch and asked what I had planned. I said I wanted to dance at one of the clubs. Randy shook his head in disbelief. "You'll need to be tough and stand up for yourself, or you'll end up in the gutters. And you won't survive very long on these streets."

For a moment, I hesitated, but I wanted to start a new life and I knew in my heart that everything would be okay. I reached for his hand across the table. "Thank you for everything you've done for me," I said. "You believed in me when I didn't believe in myself and gave me another chance at life. I'm truly grateful for your act of kindness. If it weren't for you, I'd probably still be going down the same destructive path. I could never thank you enough for all you've done. How can I ever make it up to you?"

Randy's normally stoic face was heavy with emotion. "I don't want anything from you," he said. "The greatest gift would be to know you stayed off drugs. I hope you'll become the strong, happy person you are in Vegas every day."

He looked down at our hands, still entwined, as he spoke. "You have a heart of gold, Naomi. I saw the good in you from the beginning. If I hadn't, I wouldn't have kept helping you. I've seen drug addicts before and usually, there's no hope for them, but I saw your sincerity and determination."

Randy wiped away his tears and smiled. "I'm glad I was able to help you."

"I hope one day I'll be able to do the same for someone else," I said.

He stood up and hugged me. "Please take care of yourself, and don't be a stranger."

"Thank you, Randy. I'll be in touch."

Lance left work early to pick me up. I was nervous, but as soon as we saw each other it was as if I'd never left. We got along well, and I could be myself around him. I felt like the luckiest person in Vegas even though I only had two hundred dollars to my name.

We went straight out to explore. Vegas was magical. Everywhere I looked, there were tourists, street performers, girls in sexy outfits trying to get people into the casinos, street hustlers, and people begging for money. Once an hour, there was a light show on Fremont Street. I felt like a kid again.

The next day, I went to work with Lance at Aladdin Timeshare Tours. I was his greeter for the day, standing outside waiting for couples to walk by so I could lure them in and he could sign them up for tours. Two guys stopped and asked me how much. At first, I wasn't sure what they meant, but then I realized they thought I was a prostitute. "No, thank you," I replied loudly. "I'm not a hooker." I glared at them with disgust. They looked embarrassed and apologized as they walked away. Being a hooker was the last thing on my mind. I wanted to stay away from that lifestyle.

That first week in Vegas, I didn't do much besides work with Lance, watch movies, and get used to my new surroundings. Lance was blown away by how few movies I'd seen. He and his roommate offered me the small coat closet in the hallway for privacy. Even with my few belongings, it was uncomfortable and crowded.

The following week, I stood in front of the mirror at the Spearmint Rhino, getting ready for my first shift. The dressing room was huge and filled with dancers. I tried saying hi to some of them. I had so many questions, but no one was interested in talking to me. I realized I was on my own and had to put on my big girl panties to make it there. I got dressed and went out onto the floor, ready to work. The Spearmint Rhino was such a big place that it seemed impossible that I'd ever get used to it. All the other girls looked comfortable, talking to customers and giving them dances. I felt lost. The DJ asked what name I wanted to use.

"Rebecca," I said.

"Rebecca is already taken."

I kept choosing the girl next door Amish names like Emma, Melinda, Rachel, and Susan, but they were all taken. I thought I'd use my real name, but that was also unavailable. "How is it possible that every name I choose is already being used?" I asked.

"You can be Rachel today until you think of another name because the other Rachel doesn't come in until later." He said there were a few girls before me, but he'd get me on stage soon. Although I hadn't danced in a long time, I was excited because they had a tall pole and I liked doing pole tricks.

Going on stage was like riding a bicycle. I hadn't forgotten my tricks. AC/DC's "Hells Bells" came on, then "Back in Black." As I climbed the pole, I came alive. I did my flips and inversions, spreading my legs as I slid back down. A customer sitting near the stage clapped and put twenty dollars in my thong. It felt so great to be on stage again, and I made a little over two hundred dollars. Not bad for my first day dancing in Vegas.

For a while, I had a different name every day. Sometimes I had two or three names in one day. On the weekends, more than three hundred girls were working at once, and it became a joke between the DJ and the regular customers because we had to figure out what name I'd use.

123

Finally, one of the dancers approached me.

"Are you ready to have your own name?" she asked.

"Yes, actually," I replied. "I'd love to have my own name."

"The customers are joking about it. Nobody can keep track of what to call you. I'm Francesca, at least for now. Come on, let's find you a name."

She led me back to the dressing room, pulled a baby name book from beneath a pile of underwear and began calling them out. I didn't like any of them. She was all the way to the R's when she put the book down. "Okay, you're being too picky, and that's why you don't have your own name yet."

"None of those names fit my personality."

Francesca looked up from the book and smiled. "Okay," she said dramatically. "This is it. Risa. It means laughter in Spanish. You're so happy and bubbly. Risa fits you perfectly."

I shook my head, rejecting it immediately. "I've never even heard of that name," I said.

"Exactly. That's why it's perfect for you. And you'll finally have your own name."

"I hate it."

"Too bad," Francesca said. "It's a cute name for a cute girl, and you'll grow into it before you know it."

That's how I ended up with the stage name Risa.

I felt so awkward when I introduced myself to people as Risa. Most guys misheard me and called me Lisa. Then I'd say, "It's Risa, like Lisa but with an R." It ended up being a great way to start a conversation. It took a while, but I grew to like my stage name.

I started working more so I could buy a car. Rowan kept calling to tell me that he and Dan couldn't afford to eat. Still steeped in guilt for moving away, I wired them some money. When Rowan called and asked for two thousand dollars to fix the truck I left behind so he could sell it for me, Lance warned me not to fall for it. He was certain Rowan was taking advantage of me. We got into a huge fight over it. In the end, I didn't listen to Lance. I thought he was trying to control me, and I sent

Rowan the money. Lance told me I'd never see it again, and he was right. I was so disappointed that I argued with him when he was trying to save me some heartbreak.

That was it. Lance told me I wasn't allowed to have contact with Rowan and Dan. He insisted that I call and tell them they were losers and not to call me again. I was pissed but did as he asked. Not talking to Rowan anymore was fine with me. With the crack fog lifted, I realized we had nothing in common.

Once in a blue moon, I called Dan. He was always delighted to hear my voice and talked about how much he wished he could see me. It was depressing, and we stopped speaking for a few years. I later realized I might not be alive if it weren't for Dan, so one day, I picked up the phone and called him again. He was so surprised to hear my voice. After that, I called him once a week until he died from sepsis.

Having my own money gave me confidence again because I could finally support myself without selling my body or relying on anyone. I loved the new me, but I wasn't satisfied working at Spearmint Rhino. I wanted to work at a better club and make more money.

Then I got hired at Cheetahs. The vibe was more laid back, there were fewer dancers, and they were nicer than the dancers at the last club, so I felt at home. I quickly made friends, which is exactly what the new me craved. Unlike Spearmint Rhino, I fit right in. Cheetahs was everything I'd imagined and hoped dancing in Vegas would be. The house moms checked us in at the beginning of each shift and ensured everything operated smoothly in the back. They made sure we wore two pairs of panties as required by local law, and plenty of jewelry. At first, I didn't like the extra layers, but I felt more protected in the end. Sometimes the house moms brought us home-cooked meals. All we had to do was tip them.

Helen was my favorite house mom, taking me under her wing and showing me the ropes. She was patient and kind, and her strong English accent was comforting in the dressing room after a long shift. She asked how I was doing and if I needed anything. While I never told her about my old life, somehow, it felt like she already knew.

No matter what, Helen's hair and makeup were always impeccable. I'd never worn much makeup because I didn't know how to apply it, but Helen showed me how—and wow, what a difference! When she finished, I looked at a new woman in the mirror. Long dark eyelashes framed my blue eyes, emphasized with black eyeliner. My eyebrows were perfectly groomed and golden. Rosy blush heightened my cheekbones, and pink lipstick brightened my mouth. I gasped as we both looked at my reflection. "I look so beautiful," I whispered.

Helen turned away from the mirror and leaned over, cupping my face in her hands. "Naomi, you were already beautiful. Maybe this will help you see it."

When I first moved to Vegas, I went into a store for exotic dancers and bought a couple of skirts with unflattering tops off the clearance rack because that was all I could afford at the time. Helen brought in racks of homemade dance clothes to sell at the club and helped me pick out booty shorts and bikini tops covered in studs and sequins in hot pink, purple, and lime green. When I put on one of Helen's outfits and did my makeup, I looked in the mirror and no longer felt shy. I held my head high as I strutted through the club. Compliments started pouring in from customers, boosting my confidence to another level.

My new identity was so different from the old me in Michigan. I was proud of myself and who I was becoming instead of feeling ashamed and wanting to hide. I felt seen and loved. The light in my soul was lit, and I realized it was my time to shine.

My goal was to get the customers to the VIP room because that's where dancers supposedly made the big money. Two weeks into the job, I succeeded. I began by dancing with my back towards the customer, shimmying up and down just out of reach. When I turned around, his pants were unzipped, and his penis hung out. Shocked, I tried to cover him up and asked him to put it away. What did he think would happen with a bouncer standing there?

He said nothing, just zipped up his pants, gave me some extra money, and walked out. "Uh oh," I thought. Is this what happens in a Vegas VIP room? Do the other dancers allow this and do the bouncers turn a blind eye for an extra tip? It was certainly against the club rules. I just stood there not knowing what to do, wondering if I should tell the bouncer, but the customer had already left and I was just glad he paid me. Later I discovered that someone was always monitoring the cameras, and dancers got fired if they touched a guy's penis or allowed anyone to touch them.

Customers asked me out all the time. At first, I told them that I didn't know them well enough—but some men came in more often thinking if they got to know me, I'd go out with them. I stood my ground and always had an excuse. One of the dancers suggested I tell them that I only date women. My goodness, that was brilliant! It worked most of the time. Sometimes, I met guys determined to change my preference. The hardest part was remembering what I told each guy. It became a game to me.

I finally began to feel settled in, and everything was going smoothly with Lance. I bought a car, and we went to live shows on the Strip and did touristy things to keep life interesting. It felt exhilarating to go out and be social instead of being stuck in a smoky, run-down motel. I became a social butterfly who enjoyed going out and meeting new people. Lance and I held hands everywhere we went. He seemed proud of me and showered me with compliments. It was easier to breathe, and I felt lighter when I walked. I started coloring again, which I enjoyed doing as a child. Life felt like an adventure, as I'd imagined it would when I moved.

Lance introduced me to the Burning Man festival in 2004, an annual party in the northern Nevada desert. He also brought a new drug for me to try and, during the long drive to the festival, I smoked crystal meth for the first time. Meth kept me awake and energized, but I was glad when we ran out just before arriving. I'd seen what it did to some of Lance's friends, and it reminded me of being a crackhead.

As we looked for a place to camp, a man began waving to us from a scaffold, then jumped down, buck naked, and motioned for me to get out of the car. I did, and he picked me up and swirled his penis in figure eights as he danced with me cradled in his arms. Though taken aback, I soon learned this was not an unusual greeting at a Burning Man festival. Many people walked around completely naked, open and free. Lance hadn't told me much about it, and we were unprepared for the natural elements of the open desert. When the dust and wind picked up, we could barely see. I wrapped one of Lance's bandanas around my face and carried a blanket around at night because I hadn't brought enough warm clothing. Most people were dressed outrageously in fur coats and glitter platform shoes or bikinis with combat boots and glitter eyelashes. LED lights twinkled from their hats, coats, and glasses.

During the day, while it was warm, I walked around wearing only a thong. I was grateful that Lance suggested we bring a bicycle because once we found a camping spot, we weren't allowed to drive. Although I disliked the wind and dust, I soon forgot all about the outside world and felt freer than ever. One evening, I smoked a joint while riding a bicycle and kept falling over. Before I knew it, a bunch of people came up behind me and pushed me along. We talked and joked as they guided me to their camp, where we danced for hours. Random people kept offering all kinds of drugs: ecstasy, molly, LSD, weed, and hash. I was high for most of the week and didn't sleep much. At night, the art cars and sculptures illuminated the Playa. There were very few rules at Burning Man. It was an indescribable feeling of freedom I'd never experienced anywhere else.

It was hard to return home to the real world of rules and laws. For the first two weeks, I slept a lot to allow my body to recover. I sprained both of my ankles from dancing so much. During the last few days of the festival, I felt some pain but didn't realize how bad it was until we drove home. I had to take four weeks off work so my body could heal.

The only thing I disliked about being a dancer was when people asked what I did for a living. I often lied and told them I was a bartender or waitress because I didn't want to feel judged or make them uncomfortable. Occasionally, I felt empowered and didn't care what they thought. It took me a long time to realize that I'm not responsible for people's feelings. But for now, I had to come up with something to tell my family about what I did for work. I was overdue for a visit, and they were bound to ask.

The answer came to me while watching a magic show on the Strip. The next day, I wrote my family a letter telling them I was a magician's assistant in a big magic show. Perhaps I should've thought it through because they had many questions when I finally did visit. No one in my family had ever been to a magic show, so they were in disbelief. I described some of the acts I saw and explained how they were performed to the best of my knowledge. My favorite story was the one where I supposedly lay in a box and the magician stabbed knives through without hitting me. The looks on their faces were priceless. I felt bad for lying, but I honestly didn't think they'd ask so many questions. Telling my Amish family that I was a stripper would've been worse. Even so, they worried about me getting hurt in the knife act. I practiced telling the magic act story, and it became a fantasy to learn more. I ended up studying magic and enjoyed talking to my family about the magic show I was never really part of.

I quickly got used to working at Cheetahs, but only when I needed money. Before long, I made friends with Venus, another dancer at the club. Venus was cute and tiny, only four-foot-nine inches tall, with dirty blond hair that fell just below her shoulders. Her smile and voice were equally adorable. Guys often asked if we were sisters.

Venus and I held hands and approached customers asking if they wanted a "double-decker pecker-wrecker." That always made them laugh, and we had a lot of fun performing together.

Venus introduced me to a well-known Vegas attorney named Adrian Kester when he and his buddies came to Cheetahs looking for a good time. We danced for them, and they invited us back to Adrian's house. Venus assured me he'd pay us to have a good time, but I was hesitant because of Lance. I hadn't done anything like that since we started dating. I wondered if he'd break up with me or if I should tell him at all. There were so many questions. Venus insisted it was worth my time and that nothing bad would happen. She warned me not to tell Lance, but I insisted I had to, although I'd wait until afterward.

Venus invited two other dancers, and the four of us drove to Adrian's huge house on a hill overlooking Vegas. We had a few drinks, took off our clothes, and got into the hot tub by a glowing swimming pool.

Adrian pulled Venus onto his lap. She wrapped her legs around him and they made out while the rest of us watched. Excitement trickled down my legs, and I wanted to join in. When Adrian looked at me and held out his hand, I floated toward him and occupied his other side. Adrian moved his mouth from Venus's to mine and slipped one finger into each of us. I could tell because we both moaned at the same time. Venus turned my face to meet hers, and we kissed while Adrian rubbed our breasts and another woman wrapped her lips around his erect cock. He threw his head back and fully embraced the blow job as the fourth woman joined in, gently urging my legs open as Venus turned and arched her back so I could go down on her.

I came quickly with the excitement of my first real orgy unfolding around me. Adrian came, too, and ushered all four of us inside to his bed so we could fuck properly. He took turns with the other women, skillfully entering them and rocking them to climax as they ate me out or watched as I took turns pleasing them. I continued to engage with the other women but hung back from having intercourse with Adrian, hoping that my self-restraint would soften the blow to Lance.

It was a little after seven in the morning when I left. Lance called while I was driving home, wondering where I was, so I told him all about my night. I made seven hundred dollars and felt I barely worked for it.

Lance wasn't as excited about my night as I was. "You cheated on me?" He sounded so disappointed.

"I didn't really cheat. I only played with the girls. That's not cheating. Besides, I told you about it. You should be thankful."

Eventually, Lance dropped it but told me not to make it a habit. I defied him anyway. I didn't tell Adrian I had a boyfriend, and he didn't ask. I was starting to like him. I even thought about leaving Lance to be with Adrian, but my gut told me that a relationship with Adrian wouldn't last. Sometimes I told Lance I was on my way to work when I was really going to hang out with Adrian. I also lied about how much money I made. It wasn't fair to Lance.

At the end of 2004, Adrian invited me to Canada for a New Year's Eve ski trip with him and four friends: one guy and three other women. All expenses paid. I wanted to go but felt guilty. I asked Venus what she thought. She said since Lance and I were arguing, it would probably be a good idea for me to leave for a few days. I called Adrian and told him I wanted to go but didn't have any ski attire. He told me to go to Big Five and pick out everything I needed, then call his secretary so she could give them his credit card over the phone. I wondered why he was so nice to me, but I decided to enjoy it. I felt like a princess.

Lance was upset when I told him and begged me not to go. But my mind was made up, and there was nothing he could do about it. The rest of the week was tense. I could tell Lance was worried, but he took me to the airport. I thought, "What a nice guy, taking his girlfriend to the airport so she can spend New Year's with another man." I was so selfish. I don't know why he put up with me. He later told me he was hoping to run into Adrian at the airport so he could tell him to stay away from me. I'm glad that didn't happen; I would've been so embarrassed.

Adrian and his girlfriends met me at the terminal, and our Canadian adventure began. It was cold and beautiful, with snow-covered pine trees twinkling across the mountain. Adrian treated us to the spa, and we had a relaxing day, but I wanted to go skiing already. Everyone said it was too cold to ski: thirty below zero. That night, we got dressed up and went to a nightclub. I hadn't gone to many clubs and was intimidated by all the beautiful people. Adrian got us a table with bottle service, other people joined, and soon everyone was doing lines of cocaine. They kept asking if I wanted to do a line, but I politely declined and stayed on the dance floor for most of the night.

The next day, everyone had hangovers and said they were too tired to ski. I kept bugging them to get up, but they got irritated, insisting it was too cold. Finally, I decided to go skiing by myself. I didn't leave my boyfriend at home and travel to another country to sit around in a hotel room. I didn't care how cold it was. Once outside, I asked some other guests where I could go skiing, and they were happy to guide me. I loved being on a big adventure by myself and skied most of the afternoon. What a blast! I felt so happy, although I was a little disappointed in my so-called new friends. We didn't do much that night and flew back to Vegas the next day.

Lance looked horrible when he picked me up from the airport, and I barely recognized him. He'd lost a lot of weight and his hair was a mess. He claimed that he was unable to eat while I was gone.

We didn't talk much that night, but the next day Lance called Adrian and told him to stay away from me. Adrian agreed not to contact me anymore. I was furious and told Lance I planned to call Adrian anyway.

"Go ahead," he said. "You'll look like a dumb ass." I was ready to break up with Lance, but our lives returned to normal.

# CHAPTER ELEVEN

I met Leo during the summer of 2005 at Cheetahs. I'd never crushed so hard on a client. He was a sexy firefighter who looked like a model with neatly trimmed dark hair, dark eyes, high cheekbones, a chiseled jawline, and six-pack abs. I felt crazy butterflies every time he walked into the club. He was also charismatic, playful, naughty, and oh-so-sexy. He tugged on my hand as I walked by. "Have a shot of Patron with me."

"No way," I said but didn't pull away. "I don't drink while I'm working."

"Oh, come on! One shot won't hurt you." He kept bugging me about it, so I gave in. After one shot, I was drunk and gave him some dances.

Leo looked hungrily into my bra. "Have dinner with me at the Artisan tonight."

I turned away from him, then leaned back to whisper in his ear. "I can't."

He wouldn't quit asking and ordered me another shot. He was so sexy when he teased me. I loved it. I sat on his lap, letting my long hair hide our faces as he kissed me. It was against club rules to make out with customers. "Come to dinner with me," he whispered in my ear. "No one will find out." But I didn't want to hurt Lance again, and if he found out, he would definitely break up with me.

Eventually, though, I decided to have dinner with Leo. I told him I couldn't stay out late, and he said not to worry. We met at the Artisan and sat in a corner booth of the empty restaurant drinking wine. We couldn't stop kissing and touching each other, and while waiting for our food, he took off my shorts under the table. Lucky for him, I wasn't wearing panties. Leo slid beneath the table and crawled between my legs. He grabbed onto my inner thighs and helped himself to my waiting appetizer. I bit down on my lower lip, trying to maintain my composure as Leo's mouth made me tremble.

The poor waiter knew what we were doing but didn't say anything. When our food came, we barely ate because we couldn't keep our hands off each other. That was the longest time I've ever spent at a restaurant.

Suddenly, I thought of Lance. It was after ten o'clock, and I hadn't called him. I told Leo I had to go home immediately, but he begged me to come to his truck. I agreed while warning him that I had to go soon. We kissed, and he went down on me again, melting my resolve to leave. I felt like a rebel being so naughty in his truck. At eleven-thirty, I insisted I had to go, and he walked me to my car. I hoped he'd offer me his number, but he didn't. My emotions were all over the place. How was I going to explain this to Lance? There was no way he'd believe anything I said, and I couldn't blame him. I was getting more upset by the minute. On the drive home, I came up with a story and repeated it aloud, hoping Lance would believe it. At midnight, I walked into our condo. Lance stood there, fuming, with our roommate Mitch close behind.

"Are you okay?" Lance asked. "I was worried sick. I called the club, and they said you left at six."

"Holy cow", I thought, "he called the club." I was busted. My heart sank to my stomach.

"We even called the jails and hospitals to see if you got a DUI or were in an accident," Mitch added.

"I went to eat with a friend," I said and went into the bedroom. Lance followed me. He was furious, and rightfully so.

"Tell me exactly what happened," he demanded.

"I had dinner at the Artisan with Leo."

Oh boy, that was the wrong thing to say. Lance got even angrier. "I don't believe you," he yelled. "You're a whore. I know you had sex with him."

It didn't matter how much I tried to deny it; he didn't believe me. We argued for weeks. Finally, I couldn't take it anymore. I decided to tell Lance the truth, knowing he wouldn't believe me anyway. I had nothing to lose. I left out the details about what happened during dinner, but I did tell him what happened in the truck. It took a while for him to calm down, but he believed me. I was disgusted with myself and the choices I'd made. Part of me wanted to be free of Lance, but I craved the security of the relationship.

I was veering off course again and scared to be alone. I felt torn between two worlds. Other dancers were seeing clients outside the club and buying cars and houses. I wanted those things, too. All the temptations Vegas had to offer were right there in front of me. I also wanted to be grounded with Lance. I loved being naughty, and being with Lance kept me from going wild. And so, I stayed. But our relationship was never the same after that.

I kept thinking about Leo. Days turned into weeks, and he hadn't come into the club since our naughty night. Then one day, a waitress named Chloe marched into the dressing room with a big grin. "Oh my god, Risa, guess who's here?" I knew right away who it was.

"Is it Leo?"

"Yes, it's him. He and his buddies showed up and asked if you were here."

"Tell them I'll be out soon." I trembled as I finished putting on my makeup, and it took me forever. I wondered if he still liked me. What would I say? Would I make a fool of myself? Maybe he didn't want me the same way I wanted him. So many thoughts bubbled through my head.

Throwing my shoulders back and my head up, I walked onto the floor. Leo noticed me and smiled. As I got close, he pulled me onto his lap. "So nice to see you, little hottie." He handed me a shot of Patron, we talked and laughed, and I danced for him.

"What happened when you got home after I saw you?" Leo asked.

"I told Lance what you and I did and got in big trouble."

He smiled. "I'm sorry for getting you into trouble."

"It was worth it," I assured him.

Leo continued to show up at Cheetahs every couple of weeks. Occasionally, we went out to eat., then we'd park on a quiet street where we could be intimate. I felt so alive when I was with him. When he invited me to go out on his boat, I accepted. First, I went to the club to call Lance and pretend I was at work. Then I parked at a nearby casino where Leo picked me up because I could get fired if management saw me leaving with a client.

As Leo drove to the lake, I suddenly felt awkward being with him. The drive seemed never-ending, and neither of us had much to say. When we finally arrived, I was relieved to see his friends waiting for us. I was the only girl, which was fine. I liked being the only girl. That meant I was cool, and they trusted me. Hanging out with guys and hearing them talk made me realize they didn't consider all women cool enough to hang out with them.

They put the boat into the lake, and we were off. Once we reached deep water, they started wakeboarding, and Leo suggested I try it. "No way," I said. "I'm too scared."

"I'll make sure nothing happens to you," he promised.

I didn't want to. I thought, "What if I drown or break a leg?" How would I explain that to Lance? Of course, all his friends cheered me on. I decided to go for it. After all, what did I have to lose? We only live once. I got in the water. Leo explained what I had to do, but I couldn't figure it out. The water was cold, and I felt scared. I just wanted to get back into the boat, but I didn't want them to think I was a loser, so I kept trying. Finally, I had enough and let them know I was finished. It looked like so much fun, and I wished that I was able to stand up on the board.

I continued to drink and felt pretty good, or so I thought. Suddenly, I felt really drunk and knew I was going to vomit. I told Leo I didn't feel well, and he asked if we needed to go back. "No way," I told him. I'd feel better after vomiting. I went to the back of the boat to avoid making a mess. Leo and his friends laughed, joked, and teased me about feeding the fish.

Afterward, I felt better, but I was still wasted. We met up with more friends on another boat and docked near the beach. Leo's friends on the second boat were fishing. I loved fishing! I stripped off all my clothes and swam to the other boat. The guys helped me up, asking why I was naked. I was too drunk to answer. Someone gave me his fishing pole, and I cast the line into the water. That's when I realized that my being naked was awkward for everyone. I remembered Leo telling me they were Mormons and very conservative. Suddenly uncomfortable, I handed over the fishing pole and swam back to Leo's boat, where he said I should probably put on my bikini.

We hung out by the beach for a while, then headed in. I was so wasted that I didn't even go back to the club to call Lance. I just went home. Lance asked why I didn't call him before I left the club, and I told him that I snuck out so the house mom wouldn't find out how drunk I was and refuse to let me drive. I don't know if he believed me, but I didn't care. I just wanted to sleep it off, which is what I did.

We hung out a few more times, but Leo stopped coming around the club as much. The last time I saw him, he was excited because he'd just met the woman of his dreams and wanted to get married. Then he changed his phone number and disappeared.

As soon as my fling with Leo ended, Lance got the idea that he should have more than one girlfriend and tried to convince me this would be better for both of us. I didn't understand his thought process, and we argued about it a lot. I hated the thought of him being with another woman, and he brought up the fact that I'd already cheated on him. I didn't think that gave him the right to have two girlfriends, but he convinced me that I had double standards that weren't fair, so I decided to be open to it, and we went to nightclubs looking for a woman to bring home. It became his sole mission when we went out, so much so that I couldn't enjoy myself. We took ecstasy because he thought it helped make us more social.

I was so embarrassed when he talked to other women. My energy scared them away, and Lance got angry each time we struck out. Eventually, he created a profile for me on several dating websites. I was so uncomfortable with this, but I allowed him to do it anyway, hoping we might stop arguing. While I was at work, he stayed home pretending to be me on the websites. I got a lot of responses, which he had me read aloud when I got home each day. It all felt so unnatural and wrong.

Finally, a woman agreed to a dinner date with just me. She knew I had a boyfriend, and I thought it was funny that she didn't want anything to do with him. I met her for dinner; afterward, she came to our place and requested that we be alone. Lance went downstairs and waited in his car while she and I had awkward sex. She left, and I never heard from her again.

A couple of months later, we went to an after-hours club called Drai's where Lance finally got lucky, and a young woman agreed to go home with us. I was high on Ecstasy and didn't care. The sun was already up when we got home, and the three of us went straight to the bedroom. She seemed really into Lance, but once we were naked, she crawled to me and put her head between my thighs. My body instantly responded. My legs fell open, my head dropped back, and I was soon raising my hips to her tongue. Lance moved behind her and lifted her hips so she was on her knees, then he slid underneath her while lowering her pussy to his mouth. After I climaxed, I lay there motionless as Lance entered her from behind, and they forgot about me altogether.

Maybe I wasn't in love with him anymore. My heart felt cold and detached, and I just wanted to sleep. When they were done, Lance was super happy and bubbly. He tried to be nice to me, but I ignored him, and the three of us fell asleep in our bed. When we woke up in the afternoon, she wanted a ride to her car. Things felt awkward because we were sober, and no one talked much. We never heard from her again, but Lance was happier because he finally had a threesome. It felt like our relationship became tainted after that, and I realized I didn't care about him anymore. I stayed because it felt more comfortable than leaving.

A few male employees at the club hit on me, which got annoying. I politely reminded them that it wasn't professional, and most of them stopped. But one of the DJs persisted. When I first started dancing at Cheetahs, I didn't have a car. The DJ lived close to me and offered me rides. During one of my shifts, I had a few drinks and he asked me to give him a blow job. I felt I owed him for the rides home and agreed. He led me into the DJ booth, waited until no one was looking, and guided me to my knees beneath the booth.

Announcing the next dancer, he unzipped his pants and slid his cock into my mouth. I caressed it with my tongue, making him pull out just before he came. It was quick. I didn't like to swallow, so he ejaculated into some napkins. Composing myself, I waited until he gave me the okay, then I ducked out and went back to work as if nothing had happened. I wished I hadn't done it and hoped no one saw. Lance had accused me of giving blowjobs to the DJs long before I actually did. He jinxed me. I was disappointed in myself for not saying no the first time because after that, the DJ kept asking. Since he enjoyed my blowjobs so much, I decided to tip him less at the end of my shifts. I couldn't get away with not tipping him at all, so this became our unspoken agreement.

One of the managers also kept pestering me because I'd fooled around with him and another dancer at a party outside the club one night. He didn't get to ejaculate, so whenever he saw me at work, he asked when I'd finish what we started. I tried to avoid him and detour the conversation because it made me uncomfortable. I was drunk at the party, which was separate from the club, and one good time didn't give him the right to pursue me at work. The manager began buying me drinks so he could sit and talk to me and showed me videos from our night together. "One of these days, we need to finish this in the beer cooler," he said.

I laughed awkwardly, wishing he'd forget about it. Each time I walked to the dressing room, I glanced down the hallway towards the walk-in beer cooler to make sure he wasn't there. Seeing my clients was one thing because at least they paid me. This guy had no intention of paying me. He thought he had rights over me. I wasn't sure how to tell him no, afraid he'd fire me if I rejected his advances.

Inevitably, my nightmare came true. We happened to be in the hallway together, and he insisted I finish what we had started. I decided to do it in hopes he might stop asking. We went into the beer cooler, and I gave him his blowjob. Finally, he stopped nagging. Shortly after that, he got fired, not because of what we did in the cooler, but for something he did outside the club. I was happy I didn't have to see him anymore.

My job came with perks, but it came with some danger, too. One night I left work around two o'clock in the morning, with a bouncer walking me to my car as usual. As I drove through the parking lot, I noticed a couple staring at me from inside a black SUV. When I pulled onto the road, the SUV followed. As I drove toward the freeway, I kept seeing it in the rearview mirror. My gut told me something was wrong, but I figured I was just exhausted and imagining things. Once on the freeway, I thought I lost them, but just off the exit, I noticed them again, not far behind. As much as I felt something was off, I also considered the possibility that I was overreacting. One of my neighbors had a black SUV, and I convinced myself it must be them and that I didn't need to worry.

I turned onto my street, and the SUV pulled over. Unsure where the police station was, I thought about driving to Sam's Town Casino up the road, but I was dressed skimpily and skeptical that they'd help me. I still felt unsure as I pulled up to my gate and entered the code. The SUV reappeared and drove through the gate behind me, following me to my parking spot. Then I noticed my neighbor's SUV parked in its spot. Someone else was parked in my spot, and I was at a dead end. I tried to back up, but the SUV stopped right behind me. Before I could react, a man stood at my window, pointing a gun at me and demanding I roll it down.

"Give me your purse, all your money, and your car keys, or I'll shoot you," he demanded.

"No," I said. "I don't want to." Shocked by my brief display of courage, I quickly realized it could get me killed.

He put the gun to the side of my head. "Listen carefully, or you'll die. I said to hand it over, or I'll kill you."

I was pissed at him and myself. But a few hundred dollars wasn't worth dying for, so I handed him my purse and keys.

"If you look back, I'll shoot you," he warned before jumping back into the SUV. I tried to get the license plate number, but they backed up and took off too fast. As soon as they disappeared around the corner, I grabbed my phone from my stripper bag and called 911. While on the phone with the cops, I ran upstairs and pounded on the door for Lance or Mitch to let me in. Mitch finally opened the door with a big iron rod, ready to whack someone, and Lance was right behind him with a broom. They saw me and put down their weapons.

"You scared the crap out of us," Lance said.

Since I was still on the phone, they listened to the story I relayed to the cops, pulled me inside, and shut the door. Once I hung up, they asked questions faster than I could answer. They wondered why I didn't just unlock the front door myself. Crying and shaking, I told them the thief had taken my condo keys. I was happy to be alive and grateful they didn't take the bag with my phone and all my dance clothes.

We changed our locks in the morning, but I was still scared to go out. What if they were waiting for me? I ended up buying a handgun and got a license to carry it. Honestly, I hate guns, and I was scared to have one. I couldn't help but think that it was more trouble than good and ended up keeping it at home most of the time.

After that, I decided maybe dancing wasn't for me anymore. I got licensed to sell timeshares and worked with Lance at Tahiti Village Resort, the newest timeshare in Vegas. I did okay until I was trained in sales, which felt fake, and I got bored. After nine months, I wasn't selling any timeshares, so I went back to dancing.

# CHAPTER TWELVE

Blaze was one of the best dancers at Cheetahs. Long chestnut hair fell in waves from beneath her cowgirl hat and tumbled over the top of a zip-up denim bustier accentuating her hourglass figure. The customers went wild for her knee-high boots and black booty shorts. She rewarded them by slowly unzipping the bustier, teasing them to beg for more. She'd then reveal her full, teardrop breasts while riding the pole as if taming a bucking bronco. Afterward, she greeted her regulars with massages instead of dances. She made a lot of money and owned multiple homes decorated with expensive artwork. On a slow night, Blaze pulled me aside. "Naomi, do you have any goals or dreams?"

"What do you mean?" I asked. "I work when I need money."

She guided me into a chair near the stage and sat across from me. "Can I make some suggestions?"

I shrugged. "Sure, why not?"

"Have you ever thought about buying a house instead of renting?"

I waved the idea away. "There's no way I could ever buy a house because I don't make enough money."

Blaze chuckled. "Well, my dear, that's because you don't work enough."

"I'm confused," I told her. "I work four or five days a week."

"Yes, but I only see you staying for four to six hours max. The fifty-dollar house fee you pay in the afternoon is good from eleven in the morning to eleven at night. Why not get the most out of it and make the maximum amount of money each day?" She sat back, confident that she'd made her point.

Taking Blaze's wisdom to heart, I began working more hours. Now I wanted to buy a house. The more I thought about it, I realized it was possible if I stayed focused. Pretty soon, I was unstoppable. I started making a lot of money dancing and seeing clients outside the club. In one night, I made over three thousand dollars. I became addicted to achieving my goal and stopped telling Lance how much I was making. I didn't want him controlling me anymore.

Even so, I called Lance every day when I got to work so he'd know where I was, then I'd call him before I left. He could tell I was in the dressing room because of the music in the background. If I wanted to see a client, I stopped at the club first to call him. Then I had to stop back at the club to call him again when I was heading home. I felt uncomfortable using the club as my alibi, but I didn't know how else to get away with it.

Some of my clients spoiled me with extravagant shopping sprees and sent chocolate-covered strawberries, caramel apples, and fancy cheesecakes to the club. Many wanted to go to dinner or out on the town, and I was their hot fantasy date. No drama or strings attached. Just good, clean fun.

I noticed Ben the moment he strolled into the club: tall and confident, smiling as I caught his eye. A sizeable shiny belt buckle accentuated his long legs and tight backside. His short, trim mustache and dark goatee intrigued me from beneath the shadowed brim of his black cowboy hat. After showering me with tens and twenties during my performance on stage, we headed straight to the VIP room for a private dance. The chemistry between Ben and me was electric. Even though it was against club rules, we couldn't keep our hands off each other. Keeping an eye on the bouncer, I fanned my hair over Ben's face to hide us as I lowered my mouth onto his. Hiding from the bouncers made our illicit play even hotter.

When Ben suggested we see each other outside the club, promising to take good care of me and make it worth my time, I didn't hesitate. He took me out to dinner and gambling, and we ended the night making passionate love in his hotel room.

As promised, he paid me well for my time. I felt like a princess, which felt good and wrong at the same time because I was with Lance. I wondered what Ben's story was, but I never asked, and he didn't offer. We didn't exchange personal questions, instead settling into a comfortable, unspoken routine and enjoying our time together. I tried to keep an open mind. Once he said he had to babysit his sister's kids, and I couldn't help but wonder if they might be his. But it was none of my business.

Ben wanted to try something new and suggested we go to The Green Door, a swinger's club that promised to help "consenting adults live out their wildest fantasies." We popped Ecstasy and went. I'd never been to a place like that. There were six rooms, all with different themes. We walked past the No-Wear Room, lit with black lights and draped with flowing white fabric that reflected an eerie purple hue. We could see the silhouette of a couple rocking rhythmically on a chaise lounge nearby. The woman's nails glowed in the dark as they dug into her partner's clenched buttocks, thrusting into her.

Following Ben, I was eager to see what was next. We lingered at the entrance to the dark Voyeur Room, illuminated by strings of soft green lights hanging from the ceiling. Observers lounged on long black leather sofas as couples and threesomes writhed together on platform beds. There was a room with a fountain, and another with a big jacuzzi tub. We briefly stepped into the Dungeon Room, where a man stood naked in purple faux fur handcuffs attached by a chain to the wall. When the tall woman in leather smacked his bare ass with a leather paddle, it was hard to tell if the man was crying out in pain or pleasure. Or both.

In the Orgy Room, several naked bodies entwined together on a round, red velvet bed surrounded by beaded curtains. A shiny pole for dancing stood off to the side beneath a spotlight. I looked back at Ben, who smiled, silently encouraging me to take it for a spin. I hiked up my mini-dress and grabbed the pole, lifting my five-inch heels slightly off the floor and letting my body swing into motion. Ben watched intently as I danced, and soon I captured the attention of everyone in the room.

A petite woman with long, flowing red hair looked up at me from her position on all fours on the velvet bed. Behind her, a bearlike man pulled her hips back into his pelvis, holding her there while he came. Staring at my lacy thong panties peeping from beneath my skirt, she hungrily bit her lip. Glancing flirtatiously back at her, I tugged my skirt down and went to sit next to Ben on the sofa.

The redhead untangled herself from the nude game of Twister on the bed, strolled over to me, and lifted my skirt. I didn't object. Ben shifted so I could lean into him as the woman urged my legs open. It was so different than receiving oral from a man. She teased the tip of my petals, gently moving closer to my clitoris, then used her lips and flicks of her tongue to bring me to orgasm. Instead of stopping, she kissed my inner thighs as the rush of climax passed, then she intensified again, eating me more passionately until I came even harder.

I collapsed into Ben's arms, my head thrown back, catching my breath. The woman stood up and thanked me, then walked away. "What just happened?" I asked Ben.

He leaned in and kissed my neck. "Should I have joined in?"

Waving him away, I smiled weakly. "Next time." I hadn't even had intercourse and I already felt spent. We spent the rest of the evening roaming around the club, observing erotic play at every turn.

After that, I introduced Ben to my friend, Raven, and we had many threesomes. It felt freeing to have threesomes when I wasn't jealous that I had to watch my boyfriend with someone else. Raven was a dancer at Cheetahs with a big personality and a contagious laugh. She was beautiful and curvy with big breast implants, curled shoulder-length dark hair, and dark eyes. We became best friends and partied a lot outside of work, even though she had three kids and a boyfriend. Raven loved to drink at work and strolled around the club, tipsy, in tiny black booty shorts and a black bikini top or bustier. When a client refused to pay her for dances one night, she threw a full pitcher of beer in his face.

As I came to trust Raven, I told her about my secret side gig and invited her to make extra money with clients who asked for a threesome.

Ben told me he enjoyed Raven, but no one could ever replace me and my erotic sexuality. He eventually told me he had a wife and that, indeed, those kids were his.

One of my favorite clients was a retired writer from New York named Billy. His life consisted of traveling, reading, writing, gambling, and having sex with women forty years younger than him. Billy was in his late sixties and looked just the way I imagined a writer would: skinny with a tuft of scraggly gray hair on the top of his balding head and round glasses that he cleaned with the edge of his white button-down shirt. He must've been a successful writer because he had an enormous house in the Vegas hills. After I first danced for Billy at Cheetahs, he didn't waste any time inviting me to his home for sex. He was awkward and quirky, and I felt I could trust him. He also agreed to pay me three hundred dollars for an hour of my time.

Billy made it clear right away that he didn't want to wear a condom. At first, I refused, but he offered me an extra two hundred dollars. I couldn't resist the money, and we were done in twenty minutes. I drove away with five hundred dollars for twenty minutes of work, the fastest, easiest money I ever made. Then I thought about Lance. He had no idea what I'd just done. Not only did I put my life and health at risk, but Lance's, as well. I began to panic. What would I tell him if I caught a sexually transmitted disease and gave it to him? Seriously, I felt sick to my stomach. I didn't want to go home, but I had to.

I realized Billy must be having sex with many women, and if he didn't wear a condom with me, chances were high he didn't with the others. I got tested for sexually transmitted diseases, all of which were negative. I'd never been so relieved in my life, but I continued to take the risk.

Five times a month, Billy paid me five hundred dollars for twenty minutes of my time. Each time I left his house, I worried about my decision and got tested every three months. I even had nightmares about

146

it. I also continued to risk my relationship with Lance, almost as if I wanted it to end.

Then I started seeing an older man named Curtis who limped around the club, partly from an old injury and partly from being drunk. He looked like a typical aging businessman with his neatly clipped gray hair, expensive-looking suits, and a glass of brandy in one hand. He kept asking to see me outside the club, and at first, I refused. Then one night, as I bounced playfully on his lap, Curtis offered me two grand if I'd pee in his mouth. I stood up and buried his face in my cleavage to hide my excitement. Two thousand dollars? Seriously, how bad could it be? By the end of the night, I agreed.

When the day came for me to fulfill Curtis's request, I questioned whether I could do it. Luckily for him, I really had to pee when I arrived. As usual, Curtis was drunk, but when I announced that I had to relieve myself, he perked up. He insisted that he needed to go to the bathroom first and inject medication into his penis. I winced, immediately weirded out.

He sprawled out on the sofa with his arms open. "I want every drop, baby."

I told him I didn't think he could handle every drop because I'd been holding it for a while.

"Get over here and pee in my mouth," he insisted.

"I'm going to make a mess on your nice couch," I teased him.

"It's just a couch. I'm ready!"

He leaned his head back and I straddled him. Then I let go and he drank my pee as fast as he could. As I predicted, it gushed over his face and onto the couch. It was crazy; I couldn't believe what I was doing. I started laughing uncontrollably because I'd never experienced anything like it. I asked if he wanted me to stop, but he shook his head no. He was enjoying himself. Honestly, I didn't want to stop once I started. It was one of the most empowering moments of my life.

Afterward, Curtis wanted to have sex without a condom, insisting he was free of sexually transmitted diseases. I wouldn't budge and insisted he put on a condom. I'd decided Billy was the last time I'd ever take that risk. I followed him down the hallway into the bedroom, where he took off my lace pink top and short black skirt. He asked me to lie on his bed, undressed, and put the condom on his partially erect penis. Then I climbed on top and rode him until he came. I continued to see Curtis once a week until he moved out of town. It was nice to have guaranteed weekly income.

Austin was another customer who bought a lot of dances from me and let me know he was looking for more. He said he was a criminal defense attorney and invited me to visit him at his office the next day. I asked if we needed a hotel, but he said it wouldn't be necessary. How kinky and exciting. Meeting a guy at his office for sex was a fantasy of mine, and I got hot and bothered just thinking about it.

When I arrived at the building in downtown Vegas, I was alarmed at the number of businessmen in suits milling about. How many had naughty sex secrets? Trying to keep my composure, I rode up in the old, slow elevator. The doors opened, and I was greeted by a nice-looking young woman who said she was his assistant. I hesitated. What if she told someone and I got in trouble? Maybe she knew. Perhaps it turned her on. I felt awkward because I wore a short, skintight dress with no underwear, high heels, and lots of makeup. Nervously, I told her I was there to see Austin. She didn't seem to mind. She smiled and pressed a button on an intercom to let Austin know I was there.

Austin opened the door to his office and invited me in. Once the door closed behind us, I whispered that I was uncomfortable doing anything with his assistant there. He assured me that I had nothing to worry about and went to sit in a leather chair behind his desk, silently commanding me to follow. Hiking up my dress and spreading my legs, I straddled him, and we began to kiss. He lifted me up, sat me on his desk, kneeled on the floor, spread my legs open, and ate me out. Then he took off my dress, and before I knew it, I was on the floor under his desk, just like my fantasy, giving him a blowjob. We got into it and I forgot all about his assistant. For a moment, I was grossed out by his lack of manscaping. He was hairy all over, even his back. I quickly put my feelings aside because it wasn't about me. He was paying me to have a magical time

148

and not to judge him. He groaned in pleasure but stopped me before he came.

Kneeling behind me, he anchored me on all fours and entered me. It felt good, but he was turned on and didn't last very long. I didn't mind. I loved it when clients finished quickly. That meant I spent less time with them, and my time was increasingly valuable.

Work became a great big party once I started taking Ecstasy on top of drinking. I thought I was having the time of my life, but Lance was always mad at me when I got home. He knew I was doing something but couldn't figure out what. I'd lost so much respect for him. It was hard enough to support myself, and then he expected me to support him, too. He had no problem landing a decent job, but after a few months, he'd find a way to quit or get fired. Then he'd smoke weed and watch TV. He certainly never cleaned the condo. For most of our relationship, I supported him financially, and it caused a lot of tension. Sometimes he threw things, spit on me, or socked me in the stomach. He called me bitch, slut, cunt, and a worthless piece of shit. I usually remained silent, but sometimes I called him an asshole or a dick or mumbled something under my breath, making him even angrier.

When he hit me, I threatened to call the cops, but he said they'd take me to jail because I was a liar and a slut. Part of me believed him, and the last thing I wanted to do was go to jail. He told me repeatedly that I'd never find anyone else who'd put up with me. I felt stuck. My friends at work told me to leave him, but that was hard to imagine. On the other hand, I couldn't handle it anymore. I felt used and abused, mentally and physically.

One morning that summer, I broke up with Lance over the phone on my way to work. At the club, I told Raven and Luna that I'd finally broken up with Lance. They said it was about time and invited me to a pool party with a friend of Luna's — a porn director named Ryder. With a sense of relief, I said yes. Lance called me several times that day, but I ignored him. I finally felt empowered.

Ryder was a lot of fun. He gave us ecstasy, and we hung out at the Rio Casino pool until it got dark. Then we went to the Strip to continue our night at the clubs. We stood on the back seat of Ryder's car and hung out of the sunroof, drinking beers. We went to the Tao Nightclub and had a blast dancing until the wee hours of the morning, then Luna went home, and Ryder, Raven, and I went back to his jacuzzi, where we had sex all night.

The next day, I woke to lots of messages from Lance guilt-tripping me. He said if he didn't hear from me, he'd call the police. What an idiot. I told him it was over, and I wasn't coming back. But as usual, my insecurities got the best of me, and I went home after all. "Did you have sex with anyone?" he asked.

"Yes," I said and told him all about my adventures the night before. He got jealous and angry.

"We aren't together, so I didn't cheat," I argued.

"Well, at least you're not lying to me for once."

I wanted to pack my bags and move out, but I knew Lance would stop me. "You'll never find another guy in Vegas as awesome as me," he said.

I stood there in silence as I had a flashback of my friends at work telling me Lance was abusive and had brainwashed me. Even so, I still believed in the idea of our relationship. It was a shitty feeling thinking that I might be alone forever. Sometimes I felt worthless, sure no one else would want me. I felt guilty all the time and had no self-love or confidence. I gave in and got back together with Lance.

I wished I could stay strong and move out, but I had no idea where to go and was afraid to live alone. I thought I'd be lonely and was scared I'd feel that way forever. I felt trapped. A dark cloud loomed over me like a tornado about to hit; my heart felt cold and dark, and I just wanted it to subside.

That day, I spent most of my time in the dressing room instead of out on the floor making money. When I called Lance to check in, he sounded drunk and asked where I kept my gun. I told him I didn't know, and he got angry. I was afraid he'd kill himself if he found it. Helen, our house mom, overheard my conversation and put her arm around me.

"Do not go home," she said. "It sounds like he's unstable."

"I have to," I said. "I'm worried he'll hurt himself."

Helen hugged me closer. "Honey, he isn't going to hurt himself; he's going to hurt you."

I turned away from her. "He won't hurt me," I insisted. "I'll be fine."

"Naomi, please don't go home," Helen pleaded. "You can stay with me for a while until things calm down. I have a bad feeling he'll hurt you tonight if you go home."

I thought about what she said. Sure, Lance had been violent towards me, but I'd always been able to handle it. Helen didn't give up, blocking my path as I reached for my bag. "I feel like this time is different, Naomi. I want you to think about staying with me until you figure this out."

Reaching past her, I grabbed my things. "Thank you, Helen, but I'm going home."

She looked concerned as I walked out the door. I thought she was overreacting.

When I got home, Lance was waiting for me in the bedroom. He looked really messed up and asked me again where my gun was. I chuckled and called him an idiot under my breath as I walked past him into the office. Suddenly, Lance grabbed me from behind and put a knife to my neck. "Who's the idiot now?" he yelled.

"Lance," I gasped. "Please stop. Put the knife down!" The knife nicked my skin and my survival instincts kicked in. I realized I had to fight if I was going to live. Hoping the downstairs neighbors would hear me and call for help, I screamed. Lance lifted me and dragged me by my hair while holding the knife against my neck. I tried to pull it from his grasp and wiggle away, but he gripped me harder. I wanted to knee him in the balls, but he blocked my every move. We wrestled and scrambled around the office, banging into furniture. I was determined to get away from him. Somehow, I finally knocked him in the groin and pulled the knife from his hand, slicing the tip of his finger. Blood squirted everywhere, and he ran to the bathroom yelling. "You fucking bitch! You almost cut off my finger!"

It was my only chance to get away. Screaming and hoping someone would hear me, I grabbed the knife and my spare key and bolted down the stairs. I threw the knife in the dumpster before driving off in my car. Then I broke down crying. I was in shock but happy to be alive. I'd escaped death. None of the neighbors came to help me. Certainly, someone must have heard my screams for help.

I didn't have my phone, so I pulled over to compose myself and figure out what to do next. I was battered, bruised, and bleeding. Trembling, I grabbed the pay-as-you-go phone I kept hidden in my car since I discovered Lance was monitoring my cell phone. I called my firefighter friend, Carson, but he didn't answer, so I called the cops. They asked me where Lance was, and I told them he was at the condo. They also wanted to know about the weapon. They were confused about why I threw the knife in the dumpster but said they'd send an officer to investigate. I drove back to the condo and sat in my car, waiting for the cops to show up, looking over my shoulder to make sure Lance didn't sneak up on me. After a while, I decided to check on him, left my car running, and found the condo's front door locked. I knocked and called out his name. "Maybe he died," I thought. A car door slammed behind me, and I turned around. Lance was stealing my car!

Apparently, he'd left the condo and hid nearby in case the cops came. As soon as he saw me leave my car with the engine running, he jumped in and took off. I was so pissed. I called his best friend, Darren, who asked if I'd called the cops. I admitted I had and told them the truth, then started to tell him the story. Darren cut me off. "Call the cops back right away and tell them everything is fine. Lance will be in big trouble."

Suddenly, I felt like the bad guy. I called the cops back and tried to convince them everything was okay. But the dispatcher said they had to do a welfare check. When a patrol car arrived two hours later, they refused to believe that Lance had stolen my car and accused me of protecting him. The cops kicked down the front door and searched the condo. They took pictures of the bloody scene and all the bruises on my body. One cop asked why I was protecting him. I assured him I wasn't lying; it was all a misunderstanding. He didn't believe me. I had no idea where Lance was, but I knew he was intoxicated and probably didn't get far.

Afraid he'd come back, I left in Lance's car and called Carson again, who worked at the fire station overnight. He sneaked me in through the station's back door so his crew wouldn't see me. When he stopped to look at me, tears sprang to his eyes. Blood had dried in blotches on my face, and I was still in shock. The top of my head was bleeding and swollen. He examined my cuts and bruises to ensure I was okay and offered me a shower and bed for the night. I accepted, but I couldn't sleep. Carson kneeled by the bed, gently rubbing my head as I lay awake, shivering. He cried with me, furious at Lance, urging me to follow through with the charges. "Don't worry," I assured him. "I won't let Lance get away with it." Deep down, I knew that wasn't true.

I went to Raven's the following day, exhausted and still in shock. After taking a nap, I woke up to a bunch of voice mails from Lance. Would he ever give up? Raven urged me to ignore his messages, but I couldn't resist. Lance said he was at home and badly hurt. He accused me of getting my "thug" friends to break into our condo during the night to beat him up and threatened to call the cops if I didn't return his calls. I agonized over what to do. He tried to kill me and was now turning everything around. Raven said he was trying to guilt trip me and pleaded with me not to call him.

Consumed with uneasiness, I felt overwhelmed by the urge to reach him. I blamed myself for making trouble. If I hadn't been seeing clients behind his back, maybe he wouldn't have reached his breaking point. I picked up the phone.

I barely recognized Lance's voice when he answered. He sounded weak. He said his eyes were swollen shut, and he broke his orbital bone and elbow. I assured him that I didn't hire thugs to beat him up. "Did you get into a car accident?" I asked.

"I don't think so," he mumbled.

"How did you get into the condo?"

"I don't remember," he admitted.

I kept digging. "The cops made me lock the door on my way out," I explained. "And you didn't have a key. You probably tried to climb in through the window and fell two stories to the ground."

"That's crazy," he said. "I don't remember much from last night, but I woke up broken. Please, Naomi, come home. I swear I'll call the cops if you don't, and you'll go to jail because I'm beat up way more than you."

Sighing heavily, I composed myself. "I can't come home, Lance, because I'm worried that you'll kill me."

He began to sob. "I'm so broken; I couldn't kill you even if I wanted to."

Finally, I agreed to come if someone else was there to supervise. About an hour later, his friend Darren called when he got to the condo to say that he was with Lance and that I should come home. When I got there, I called Darren and had them both come outside to see if Lance was beaten up.

I hardly recognized him. I wanted to run and scream. The horror from the previous night flashed before my eyes, and I started to cry. Lance tried to tell me that everything was okay. "I won't hurt you," he promised. I couldn't even look at him. Darren and I went downstairs to investigate my suspicions that Lance fell from the window, which he clearly had. He'd broken the bush beneath the window, and the dirt was displaced. Blood smeared the window. Lance said he didn't remember anything because he'd blacked out from alcohol and Xanax. He promised he wouldn't hurt me again, and Darren left.

I took a few days off work because I had a black eye, and my legs and arms were blotched with bruises. But after a few days at home with Lance, I was desperate to get back to work, regardless of my injuries. I covered my black eye with makeup and wore thigh-high stockings to cover my legs, but my bruises were too obvious. Helen's jaw dropped when she saw me.

She rushed over, touching my eye. "I knew he was going to hurt you."

I hung my head. "I should've listened to you." Helen hugged me for a long time.

Lance and I tried to patch things up, but nothing changed. If anything, I grew more distant. He got an attorney who managed to get charges against him dropped because I didn't want to be responsible for him having a record. I just wanted life to go back to normal, even though my normal was completely chaotic.

Despite the drama with Lance, I continued meeting new clients at Cheetahs.

# CHAPTER THIRTEEN

Oliver was a charming businessman who came to Vegas for work every other month. The first time I danced for him, I became intrigued by his huge erection. Leaning over him, I took off my pink schoolgirl crop top and flipped up the matching pleated skirt that barely covered my ass. As I danced, my black thigh-high stockings brushed over the bulge in his jeans. He gently pulled my hair and kissed my neck, sending shivers down my spine. At first, he was just a regular who turned me on. Eventually, Oliver invited me to dinner and then to his room at the Rio Hotel. As we waited in the hotel lobby for an elevator to take us to the penthouse, he suggested we wait for an empty car so he could tease me on the way up.

The elevator doors closed behind us; at last, it was just the two of us. Oliver stood behind me, his arms wrapped around my waist, kissing my neck. Warm and tingly in his embrace, I kept my eyes closed. Melting into his body, I felt his cock growing harder and straining to break free from his pants. I was so turned on that I didn't want the moment to end and hoped the elevator would take its time.

We shared a fancy, romantic dinner on the fifty-first floor in the rooftop lounge, where we could see the sprawl of Vegas stretched out below. Afterward, we went to his room. Sex with Oliver was hot and sweaty and wild. I always looked forward to spending time with him.

He called me his princess and treated me like one, taking me to high-end hotels where we watched movies, took bubble baths, and ordered room service. Sometimes he ordered couples massages for us or spa days just for me. When he wasn't working, he took me to dinner and shows, and on gambling sprees. Oliver loved having threesomes and, sometimes, he requested women from Backdoor, a website for sex workers. One woman asked for seventy-five dollars just to show up, plus whatever she charged for sex. But she was a real bitch and stank of cigarettes. Neither Oliver nor I were into her, so he paid and sent her on her way. The women who showed up from Back Door were never the women we expected. Oliver even called ahead and insisted on getting the person featured in the photos, but we never did. When I told Raven about Oliver, she agreed to join us.

Oliver loved Raven and ended up spoiling her, as well. From then on, the three of us took bubble baths, watched movies, and ordered room service together. I got to have a relaxing fun day with Oliver and then girl time, which I craved. Raven thanked me for the connection, and I said that all women should be treated like princesses now and then.

In 2010, I bought a single-story, three-bedroom, two-bath house with a two-car garage and a backyard. It was perfect for me. My heart was full of joy because I'd fulfilled a dream and I felt beyond grateful to Blaze for her words of wisdom that encouraged me to make it happen.

Lance and I moved in together. A little over a year had passed since he tried to kill me, and he still yelled at me every morning and cursed me out. My excitement and joy were short-lived because my depression took over again. I wanted to leave him more than ever because I realized he was destroying what little self-esteem I had left. I started working double shifts so I didn't have to be around him.

It wasn't long before someone captured my attention again. Jordan was tall and handsome with big blue eyes and blonde hair. Our eyes met as I walked off stage and I felt those familiar butterflies come to life in my stomach — a sure sign I was in trouble. He invited me to meet him at a pub nearby where we could gamble. By the night's end, we were back at his house having wild sex. The chemistry between us was primal. Jordan's boyish face was a contrast to his hard, muscular body. He wasted no time whipping me around and folding me over the kitchen counter. He grasped my hair with one hand while he unbucked his belt and unzipped his jeans. The clink of the metal made me shiver in anticipation. While waiting for him to undress, I took off my top and unclasped my bra. He rewarded my effort by catching my bare breasts in his hands and gently pinching my nipples. He lifted my mini skirt, yanked down my panties, and then dropped to his knees.

Kneading my bare ass with his hands, he ran his tongue up and down my throbbing lower lips. I yelled out and gripped the counter's edge, arching deeper into his mouth. He sucked on my clit until my thighs began to tremble, then he stood up and, in one swift motion, plunged his big hard dick into my already orgasming body.

We fell asleep in each other's arms. I didn't want to go home to Lance. He had no idea, and I didn't care. However, my peace of mind was short-lived. Jordan's mom lived across the street, and the next morning, when she saw my car parked outside, she stormed into the house and broke down his bedroom door. Jordan and I were still naked beneath the covers. I thought she might be a crazy ex-girlfriend until Jordan started yelling, "Mom, stop!" I wanted to run, but it was too late. She pulled the covers aside and slapped at me until Jordan grabbed her and pulled her away. He made his mom leave and apologized to me. I got dressed and went home.

Despite the drama, the following day, all I could think about was Jordan. There was no turning back. The dark cloud was dissipating, and I could see again. An overwhelming sensation of freedom overcame my body and soul. I couldn't get out of the shower fast enough to tell Lance it was over. I'd taken enough abuse for a lifetime. Time seemed to slow down as if I were swimming in slow motion through the house, trying to find Lance. It was like a dream where my legs were so heavy and tired that I couldn't move forward. But I kept moving until I saw him in the living room. I turned off the TV. "It's over," I said. "You need to get your stuff and leave, and this time I really mean it. You have a week to get out."

Lance reached for the remote to turn the TV back on. "Yeah, well, my car isn't running, and I have no money."

I snatched the remote out of his reach. "That's not my problem anymore. It's time you step up and find a way to support yourself."

Storming out of the house, I drove to work, refusing to answer his calls. He texted me that I was selfish and had no regard for human life. I told him to cry to his mom or someone who cared because I didn't anymore.

Lance continued to stay at my house, trying to be super sweet. I tried to be kind, but I no longer cared. Lance left on December first after six-and-a-half long years. Good riddance. I was happy that I finally stayed strong.

At first, I was lonely. Jordan hung out when he was available, but he was often busy with his kids. Then I remembered an old friend who'd once offered his place in California as a place to stay if I ever needed to get away, so one morning, I packed a bag and started driving. I needed some "me time." My friend was away on business, so I had the place to myself. I found peace in being alone. For five days, I went for walks on the beach, read books, went swimming, and took myself out to eat. Maybe the single life wasn't so bad after all. At least it felt like I was single because Jordan was hardly ever available. For the first time, I enjoyed my own company. It was so nice not to have to answer to anyone but myself.

Back in Vegas, I felt lost. Most of Lance's belongings remained in my house, which was a constant reminder of him. He called and made threats, claiming he hired thugs to wait outside my house. "They'll break every bone in your body," he said. Raven insisted he was trying to scare me but let me stay the night at her place a lot because I was afraid to sleep in my house. I felt guilty if I didn't answer his calls, like I owed him something. Finally, I had enough and got a new phone and number. No one attacked me, and at last, I was able to get closure and live my life again.

Life with Jordan was rocky, too. I started parking my car down the street so his crazy mom wouldn't know I was there. Even so, the drama continued. We were hanging out in his room one night doing coke when there was a loud knock on the door. At first, I thought it was his mom, but I didn't recognize the voice. Panicked, Jordan told me to crawl out the window and jump over the back fence. I refused, demanding to know what was happening, and he admitted the woman was his ex. Jordan directed me to hide in his closet and said he would talk to her. As soon as he opened the door, she walked past him right to the closet. "I know you're in there, so come on out!"

I said nothing and waited until she opened the door. Embarrassed, I apologized.

"I know he made you go in there. I'm not mad at you." She helped me out of the closet, and she and Jordan went to the living room to talk while I eavesdropped from the bedroom. "How could you do this?" she asked Jordan. I could tell he never broke up with her. How could I have been so blind?

Eventually, Jordan convinced me to go down to the local bar so he could talk to her and get her to leave. Two hours later, he told me she was gone and that I could return. He apologized and denied they were still together. I didn't care; I just wanted to party and have fun. Partying was my escape, my way of getting over Lance. Jordan was paranoid for the rest of the night, peeping through the blinds. "They're coming for me," he whispered. I asked who was coming, but he never said, just that they were outside and he had to protect us. It got so bad that I became scared for my life.

One night, I was in my bedroom watching TV when Jordan came bursting through the door holding a knife. "Come help me," he yelled. "I saw them! They're outside the house!"

I tried to get him to give me the knife, but he was determined. Looking out the windows, I saw no one. I wanted him to lie down with me, but he refused. Eventually, he went home. Relieved, I prayed he made it home safely.

I called Jordan the following day, but he didn't answer, and I began to worry. He finally called from the mental hospital, insisting that he'd heard and seen people on his roof. He took all his drugs, got his rifle for protection, opened his garage door, and lay on the floor looking through the scope of his gun. Thinking he saw an invader on a nearby roof and that the neighborhood was under attack, Jordan started shooting. The neighbors called the cops, who took him into custody without hurting anyone. Thankfully, they took him to the mental hospital instead of jail. Jordan begged me to bring alcohol and Xanax to the hospital. I told him no way. He needed to recover.

Jordan kept calling. Finally, I decided to bring him some Xanax, but the alcohol was too risky. He was trying to get released and had to be calm and behave himself. I wouldn't take any chances. I decided to stay with him until he was released if he promised not to drink or do cocaine again. When we left the hospital, it was late. "Let's go to the neighborhood bar and have one drink," he said.

Why not? It had been a long day. One drink shouldn't hurt. But one drink turned into two, and then he said, "Let's get some cocaine and celebrate." He promised to behave himself. After drinking, gambling, and doing cocaine for a few hours, Jordan was ready to go home. He told me to drop him off near his house, drive to the back street and park my car, then climb over the fence, all so his mom wouldn't see my car. Okay, I thought, "I've done crazier things than sneak over a fence." I felt safe for once, and we had a relaxing night. In the morning, I snuck out over the fence again. "How clever," I thought, and I wondered why we hadn't thought of it sooner. After that, I always parked behind his house and snuck over the fence.

Our relationship was dysfunctional and revolved around drugs and alcohol. Nothing made sense, but I couldn't stop seeing Jordan. He had lots of problems and bad habits, and I felt it was my duty to help him get better. Even so, I loved partying with him because it made me forget about my problems. I thought if he recovered, maybe we could have a lasting relationship. I never acknowledged that I might still have a problem.

Jordan and I hung out when we could, but he often flaked and stood me up. I tried to be understanding because he had two kids. On New Year's Day he texed me, saying he needed to be there for his kids and that he partied too much with me. I was only upset because he blamed me for his outrageous behavior. He was always suggesting that we get cocaine. If anything, I encouraged him to spend time with his kids. Regardless, I felt heartbroken. Raven tried to console me, but I was so sad. She even offered to help me write him an email to try and change his mind and take me back. So, I wrote that even though we weren't together, I wanted to remain friends. I invited him over for a casual dinner, no strings attached, just homemade enchiladas, and there wouldn't be any drugs in the house. Raven was sure he'd say yes, and she was right.

Jordan came to dinner and complimented my enchiladas, but it was awkward for us to be sober around each other, and he didn't stay long. I felt relieved when he left. Maybe it was better for us to go our separate ways. I decided not to contact him after that. It was up to him if he ever wanted to see me again. I knew deep down he would call when he wanted to party again. I was his escape, the fun party girl when he needed a break from life.

As I predicted, Jordan called less than two weeks later, looking for cocaine. I didn't hesitate. For the next week, we partied in a hotel room at one of the casinos, where we won and lost a lot of money. As always, our relationship revolved around alcohol, gambling, sex, and cocaine. We didn't know how to be together sober.

Jordan continued to disappear for weeks at a time. I got used to it, happy to have a break from the rock star lifestyle, knowing he'd eventually fall off the wagon again. Deep down, I wished he wouldn't. Those kids needed their dad. I felt guilty when we hung out, but he was a grown man and made his own decisions. Eventually, he ended up going to rehab. I was happy for him and hoped he'd get clean and sober for good. I'd managed to stay sober myself during that time and wanted to stay that way. Only time would tell.

After six weeks, Jordan called, insisting he missed me. I promised myself that I'd tell him it was over if he called again, but I gave in and allowed him to come by. We promised each other that we wouldn't get too messed up and went to the casino. But one day turned into two. We gambled so much that the casinos offered us complimentary rooms, making it easy to go back to the dealer to get more coke. We moved to our third casino, winning jackpot after jackpot. It felt like a dream. How was it possible to win so much money? At times, we were ahead by fifteen thousand dollars. I wanted to split the winnings and go home, but Jordan insisted we keep gambling.

After ten days, we were physically and mentally exhausted. We got lost and couldn't find our room. Then I fell asleep in the elevator, and when it stopped, I fell forward and hit my head. When we got to our room, the key didn't work. Jordan waited outside the room while I went to get a new key, but when I returned, he was gone. I walked through every floor until I found him sleeping in front of someone else's door. He slurred his words as I nudged him. "Where'd you go?"

I was so out of it and just wanted to sleep. I had an eerie feeling like I'd lost a lot of time. "Get up so we can go back to our room and sleep," I said.

He dozed off again and I started to panic. I didn't want him to get in trouble for being intoxicated. I tried to wake him, then dragged him to the elevator, hoping we wouldn't run into anyone. Jordan woke up once we got into the elevator. "Why are you being mean to me?" he groaned.

I struggled to keep him standing. "I'm trying to get you to our room."

He was too out of it to understand. We finally got inside and passed out for an entire day. When we woke up, I had a black eye and a fuzzy memory. I asked what happened and Jordan said he had no idea. Retracing our steps, I remembered the elevator incident. We'd been partying for ten days. It had to stop, or I'd end up in jail, dead, or homeless for sure. I couldn't hang out with Jordan anymore if I wanted to get my shit together.

I said goodbye and told him not to call me again. "I can't live like this," I said. I meant it. I went home, continued to sleep, and recovered for the next few days. I felt brain-dead. The thought of losing everything again was unbearable. As a crackhead, I'd lost my apartment and everything in it. I couldn't bear the thought of losing my house. I decided to take some time and rethink my life. My black eye kept reminding me of my bad choices, and I was determined not to go down that road again.

I cried, ate, and slept so my body and mind could recover.

A few days before my thirty-first birthday, a friend from the past texted from California to say he was coming to town for work and wanted to take me out for drinks. I'd met Blake two and a half years earlier at Cheetah's while he was in Vegas for a convention. He was tall and slender with icy blue eyes, and a unique haircut that made him look like a rock star. His laugh was unforgettable, and he was the life of the party.

Our connection was magnetic from the moment I walked out of the VIP room and saw him for the first time. He was walking towards the door to leave when our eyes locked, and we made a beeline for each other. We met in the middle, and without saying a word, we hugged, his hard-on pressed into my stomach. He wanted me to dance for him but only had a few more minutes because he was catching a flight back home. We exchanged email addresses, and I never stopped thinking about him.

While I was excited to get Blake's text, I politely told him I wasn't feeling well. My black eye hadn't fully healed, and I was embarrassed to see him like that.

"No problem," he said. "I'll be back next week."

I felt relieved. I didn't want to miss seeing him and discovering if we still had feelings for each other. I still got tingly when I thought about him.

Blake came back the following week. By then, I was feeling more like myself and couldn't wait to meet up with him. I wore a slinky black dress and matching heels with zippers on the backs. Blake's head turned as soon as I walked into the bar. As our eyes met, his face relaxed into a familiar smile. I couldn't help but laugh a little, letting out some of the excitement I'd been holding in. He stood up and hugged me, and I immediately felt the magnetic draw toward him.

Within minutes, it felt as if he'd never left. We went back to his hotel room, made passionate love four times, and cuddled all night. We hardly knew each other, but when he gazed into my eyes, it felt like our souls had merged. I wished the night would never end and I could spend the rest of my life wrapped in his arms. Before he left Vegas, Blake bought me a plane ticket so I could visit him in California the following weekend.

I loved southern California Being there felt so right, and within a few hours, I didn't want to go back to Vegas ever again. I felt like Blake and I were supposed to be together, that he was the missing piece of a puzzle waiting to make me whole. With Blake, I felt alive and free. The music and underground warehouse parties he took me to were so different from the clubs in Vegas. I immediately fell in love with the music. It soothed my soul and made my heart dance.

I returned home and continued my classes at the community college, but Vegas was no longer fun for me. I just wanted to be with Blake in California. I started driving to see him twice a month and stayed for a week each time. I felt at home there, and we started talking about living together.

Early on, I made a fateful mistake by lying to Blake about seeing clients outside the club. I wanted to tell him, but worried he'd break up with me. I realize now it was selfish, and I should've been honest with him from the beginning. I was traveling back and forth so much that I wasn't making enough money at the club, so I fell back into what worked for me in the past. Every day, I carried the horrible secret. I wanted to have an honest relationship for once, but I crushed that dream early on. I couldn't help myself. All I saw were dollar signs.

# CHAPTER FOURTEEN

Back in Vegas, I began seeing Evan, a local high-profile criminal defense attorney. He became my favorite client: handsome, polite, well-dressed, and he smelled delicious. Sex with Evan was kinky, fun, and well-paid. He confided in me about his wife and his suspicions that she secretly fantasized about other women and asked if I'd meet her without letting on that I already knew him. We came up with an idea to make her fantasies come true and planned it very carefully. Evan told me regardless of what happened, he'd give me a thousand dollars for my efforts. I had to admit I was nervous.

Evan texted me that he and his wife would be at the Green Valley Ranch Casino, where I found them sitting at the bar. I made a beeline for the open seat next to Evan's wife, Natalie, and sized her up. She twirled a strand of her chestnut brown hair as she gazed up at her husband. They were still in love. Feeding the slot machine on the bar, I waited for my drink and made small talk with Natalie. We hit it off right away. I told her I was supposed to meet my girlfriend, but she flaked. Natalie was intrigued, and I began to flirt with her, complimenting her eyes and leaning in to touch her hair. Evan watched as I ran my fingertips up his wife's thighs, and she responded by parting them slightly. Leaning in, I kissed the bare skin where her neck met her shoulder. Natalie glanced at her husband as if to get his permission before accepting my kiss on her lips. Ever so gently, I encouraged her lips to part and her tongue to meet mine. Once we were making out, it was hard to stop.

When we paused to order another round, I asked if she was alone and Natalie introduced me to her husband, Evan. At that point, I apologized to him for kissing his wife. He flashed a huge grin and said it was fine with him. He was thrilled that his wife was having a good time.

"You have my full permission to do what you want with her," he announced, raising his drink to toast us. Natalie and I went to the bathroom together, kissing some more. I complimented her the whole time, ensuring she felt confident and comfortable before returning to the bar, where I showed no interest in Evan. I apologized for ignoring him, but he assured me he was fine.

After a couple more drinks, Natalie asked if I wanted to join them in their hotel room. I told her I'd be honored, and we held hands as we walked. Evan held the front door open for us as we continued to kiss and move toward the bed. I climbed on top of her as she ran her fingers through my hair. I gently kissed her neck and opened the buttons of her blouse. Her heavy breathing turned me on. I flung her blouse to the side, caressed her breasts, then unzipped her skirt and took it off. Slowly making my way down to her thong, I gripped it with my teeth and pulled it down to her ankles. I caressed her thighs and put my hand gently on her silky-smooth lips. She moaned as my finger entered her. Evan sat next to us, stroking his big, beautiful cock. My tongue rolled over her hard clit as her moans got louder until she orgasmed. After a moment, she looked at me and began to giggle. It was an awkward moment because Evan was sitting next to us with a big erection, but I continued to focus on Natalie. Evan didn't touch me. Instead, Natalie returned the favor and ate me out until I quivered.

After a few hours of fun, I decided to leave so I wouldn't wear out my welcome. Before I left, Natalie and I exchanged numbers. She asked where I worked, and I told her about Cheetahs. "We love that place," she said enthusiastically. "We've known the general manager, Dakota, for years!" She said they would come to see me sometime.

The following weekend, Evan and Natalie came to the club and took me to the Half-Hour Room, where I danced for her. I could tell Natalie liked me but also felt a little jealous, so I never did anything sexual with Evan in front of her. They invited me back to their suite at the Artisan Hotel, across the street from Cheetahs. Natalie and I had sex again, but I could feel the tension. I tried to make her feel comfortable, but I couldn't. So I left. Evan and I later realized she wasn't into it anymore, and he stopped setting up dates for the three of us.

Despite my secrets, Blake and I were happy. I continued to visit him in California, and when he traveled for work, which was often, he allowed me to tag along. I loved going on trips with him. His employers put him up in nice hotels, and while he was working, I explored the city. We were in love, and everything worked out in our favor.

We had a lot of sex, even when sharing hotel rooms with his coworkers. While in Ventura, we stayed in a hotel on the pier and I walked the beach, collecting rocks and beach glass. I watched people flying kites over the shoreline, and it looked fun, so we found a kite shop and bought a rainbow kite for me and a black one for Blake. We enjoyed flying our kites that night. The next day, I took my kite to the beach, where I saw a unique orange and cream-colored rock. I was so fascinated that I forgot about the kite and accidentally let go. Grabbing the rock, I chased after my kite with the wind carrying it faster than I could run. I tripped over my feet as the kite flew further away. Finally, I gave up, sure it was gone forever. I felt like crying. I stopped running, caught my breath, and saw the kite hovering close to the hotel. Maybe some nice person would grab it and hold it for me until I got there. As I got closer, I realized the kite string was stuck to a fence. I couldn't believe my luck.

Once I had my kite back, I realized I no longer had the rock. I must've dropped it when I fell down chasing after my kite. In the end, I was happier that I had the kite instead of the rock. Sometimes I flew the kite outside the window where Blake worked, hoping he'd see it and look out. But he was so focused on work that he never noticed. I enjoyed flying my kite even if he didn't notice me. I was happy just being close to him.

I continued to travel between Vegas and California for over a year and a half before officially moving there. By the end of 2012, I decided I couldn't drive back and forth anymore, and it was time to upgrade my lifestyle. I moved in with Blake, planning to get my X-ray technician, Phlebotomy, and Medical Assistant licenses. I could see the light at the end of the tunnel. I could have a better future by dedicating one year of my life to school.

Going to school was intense. Suddenly, I had to study for tests and quizzes. Blake and I were still going to clubs several nights a week, and I quickly realized I had to focus and study to succeed. The textbooks were huge. Early on, I discovered how to study and skim over the critical points of the material that would most likely be on the tests. I kept telling myself it was only a year.

I continued traveling to Vegas one weekend per month to make enough money to support myself. Somehow, I survived and graduated with high honors a year later. Finally, I'd earned a professional academic degree, a huge accomplishment that I was proud of.

Feeling confident and on top of the world, I celebrated by having a party. At last, I wouldn't have to dance or see clients anymore. Shortly after graduation, I got hired as a phlebotomist at a doctor's office. I was so excited to have a big girl job. All the hard work I put into school was paying off. I loved the work, but the three-hour-a-day commute got old, and I only made eleven dollars an hour. Once again, I realized that I had to find a way to earn more income. I'd just spent twenty thousand dollars going to college, yet I wasn't able to support myself financially doing the work. I felt let down because the system was clearly broken. I wondered how other people made ends meet doing these jobs. Dancing wasn't an option for most people. I realized people are slaves to their bills and wondered when they had time to enjoy their lives. I didn't mind working, but not for pennies.

I tried for six months but failed to support myself on my phlebotomy income. Every few months, I drove to Vegas, and for two days, I saw as many clients as I could without ever going to the club. I set appointments starting at eight in the morning and sometimes saw fourteen guys in two days. By the end of the day, I was so exhausted that I just wanted to crawl under a rock and cry. It was the only way I knew how to support myself financially. I never asked Blake for money. I wanted to support myself and not rely on anyone else. But by the end of two days, I was overwhelmed and couldn't wait to return to California. Each time, I hoped that I'd never have to go back to Vegas again, but then I ran out of money, and I'd plan another dreadful trip to Vegas.

It was hard to face Blake after seeing fourteen clients. I hated leaving him, but I made more money in two days there than I made in an entire month as a phlebotomist. I decided to stick with my big girl job because I liked the people I worked with and enjoyed drawing blood. I also figured it would look good on my resume to stay at the same job for a few years.

After two years of working at the doctor's office, I made my first attempt to quit. Devastated, my boss asked what it would take for me to stay. I thought about it, but I wanted my freedom back. I missed having control over my schedule and income. Dancing was so much easier. At first, I offered to stay if they gave me a raise, which they did. I was a little happier for a while, but the drive was still killing me, and I started looking for a job closer to home. I interviewed for a few phlebotomist positions, but they all started at eleven dollars an hour. It was infuriating to have paid so much for college and still be unable to find a decent-paying job, especially in southern California. I tried to come up with a plan to be free, and the only answer I could come up with was dancing. All that hard work in school would be wasted.

Blake pushed me to stay at the phlebotomy job, reminding me how proud of me he was. He still had no idea I was seeing clients in Vegas. Some days I cried while driving to and from work. I felt stuck in a never-ending loop.

Another year went by, and I got introduced to a network marketing company where there was potential to earn more money. Still, with my regular job, it was impossible to catch up. Finally, I gave the doctor my two-week notice so I could focus my energy on the network marketing company. I felt instantly empowered. If it didn't work out, I could always go back to Vegas.

After I quit phlebotomy, I spent a lot of time and money trying to make a living with the network marketing company. It was a waste. I loved the products, but they were expensive and hard to sell. Once again, Vegas came to the rescue. This time, I stayed for four or five days at a time, so I made more money and was able to relax. Despite my efforts to change my career, being a dancer gave me endless freedom and fun. It made me realize my true passion. On stage, I felt free, empowered, and confident. But I also took risks that put my life in danger.

One evening at Cheetahs, I met a pro football player visiting from Texas with three of his friends for his birthday. After giving them a few dances, they invited me to go back to their room at Trump Tower. I explained my rule: I don't leave the club with customers, but they insisted that it would be quick and painless; all I had to do was dance. I'd heard that many times before and wasn't falling for it. Besides, I had a bad feeling they might be cops, and I wasn't about to get arrested for prostitution. I asked if they were cops. They all laughed and said I was being weird. I didn't care what they thought about me. I told them I would think about it and let them know.

I moved on to other guys and continued dancing. When I went on stage, one of the football player's friends came to the edge of the stage to tip me and asked me to give the birthday boy another dance. I agreed, and while I performed a little striptease, he asked again how much for a private dance in the hotel room. I reminded him there would be no sex, and he assured me he understood the rules. I told him it would be four hundred, no sex. "Deal," he said.

On my way to Trump Tower, I was a nervous wreck thinking about being alone with these guys. No one knew where I was going. Seriously, what was I thinking? They could kill me and dispose of my body, and no one would ever know where I was or what happened to me. I shook so much that I had difficulty holding on to the steering wheel. I eventually pulled over to call and let them know I was too scared to come. They assured me they were just "good ol' boys from Texas" looking to have a good time. Besides, they pointed out, there was too much security at Trump Towers for anything bad to happen. I thought about the money they offered and remembered that's what I came to Vegas for, so I decided to suck it up and go.

One of the guys met me in the lobby and escorted me to the room where they were drinking. They seemed mellow, but I decided not to drink to stay in control. After some conversation, the birthday boy said he was ready. I asked if he had the money we agreed on, and he promised to pay me before I left, so I started dancing for him. Honestly, it felt weird and awkward, but I was there to do a job, and that's what I did. I stripped down to my thong, and the guys shouted and whistled. Then the birthday boy said he wanted to share and directed me to dance for his three friends. They quickly got friskier. The birthday boy had me go into the bedroom with his friend, insisting he would "take care of me" if I "took care" of his friend. His friend had a condom, and I again reminded myself why I was there, so I agreed, and we had quick sex. When he was done, he went back to the living room, and I took a shower. When I left the bathroom, another guy sat on the bed waiting for me. At first, I wanted to say, "No way! That wasn't part of the deal." But the birthday boy had said he would take care of me. I had sex with the second guy and took another shower, only to find the birthday boy waiting for me this time. I thought, "Is this really happening? Are they really running a train on me?" I wanted to cry, but I kept thinking it would be worth it for the money I'd get, and at least they were letting me take a shower in between. I felt used and abused but also thought, "What's the difference?" Some days I had sex with seven different clients and had to drive from place to place. Tonight, they all happened to be in the same bedroom. I justified it by being grateful that they weren't hurting me physically. I hadn't yet realized how low I'd set the bar for myself or that I deserved better.

The birthday boy was doing me doggy style when he announced that he always wanted to cum on a woman's face. I wasn't thrilled with that, but I allowed him to do it. I wanted to vomit. I was so grossed out and upset with myself. Why had I agreed to this? I felt so belittled, like he was looking for revenge with that final demand. I regretted allowing him to do that. Then I remembered there was one more guy. Sure enough, I came out of the shower to find the fourth guy lying on the bed waiting for me. I was so over it. I just wanted to leave already, but I let it happen, feeling powerless to say no. When I told him to make it quick, he argued that it wasn't fair and that he'd take as long as he wanted. Thank goodness he made it quick after all. I took one last shower and got dressed. Everyone was asleep except the birthday boy. I asked for the money he owed me so I could be on my way, and he handed me four hundred dollars.

Disgusted, I threw it in my purse. "What happened to taking care of me like you said you would before I had sex with all your friends?"

He claimed it was a lot of money and all he had. Sitting back down, I demanded another four hundred, or I wouldn't leave.

"Good luck. Your price is too high," he said. He wouldn't budge, and I snapped.

"Do you realize I just fucked you and your three unattractive buddies for four hundred dollars?" It felt like I was being robbed. I was so pissed at him, but I was also disappointed in myself because I didn't collect the money when I first got there. Ultimately, I felt it was my fault because I knew better to always collect the money upfront. That night, I learned a valuable lesson and promised myself I'd never make that mistake again. Thank goodness they didn't rape or kill me.

That spring, Blake and I got tickets to a huge Easter party where we met a young woman named Keisha. I watched Blake lift her up until her feet dangled off the floor as they giggled and kissed. I finally got his attention and pulled him to the side.

"Stop being so friendly with her," I hissed.

Blake tried to put his arm around me. "But she's so adorable," he replied. "I can't help myself."

Rolling my eyes, I reminded him that she was barely eighteen. "She acts like a child and you love it. I want to leave."

Blake insisted we stay, and I realized leaving wouldn't fix anything. Blake went out by himself all the time, and he'd probably run into Keisha again. She clung to him for the rest of the night, and I decided to become her friend in hopes she would be respectful and not encourage him to cheat on me. I got her number and planned to stay one step ahead of them. Keisha begged us to invite her home with us. I had to work the next day and Blake didn't, so that meant they'd be home alone. I wasn't okay with that and repeatedly told her no. They were both upset with me, and the next day, Blake was furious.

"I really wanted to have sex with her," he complained. We argued about her quite a bit, which was annoying. I had no idea that Blake had her phone number until he left his phone in the garage, and I suddenly had an overwhelming urge to go through it. The first messages I found were all from Keisha, and it was clear they were more than friends. Furious, I started to cry, realizing I had to confront him.

When Blake walked into the garage, I began screaming about Keisha. He denied everything and called me crazy. He was mad at me for snooping through his phone, turning everything around, so the fight became about me snooping instead of him cheating. He said I violated his trust and privacy and that nothing happened. He and Keisha were just friends.

I didn't believe him. "Call her right now and tell her you can't talk to her anymore or I'll break up with you."

Blake smirked. "You have nowhere to go. Good luck."

He refused to call but promised he would stay away from Keisha.

I was devastated and kept thinking about what Lance told me — that one day a guy would treat me the way I treated him. He said I'd get my karma. His words haunted me, and I cried for many days. Blake said he loved me and didn't want to be with anyone else, but I couldn't believe him. I knew what I read in the text messages. He said that I was pushing him away by being so insecure.

I just wanted our lives to go back to normal, but our relationship was never the same after that. I constantly tried to get a hold of his phone to snoop some more, but he never let it out of his sight. I justified my own cheating because I was doing it to support myself financially.

About six months after I discovered the text messages, I found naked pictures of Keisha in Blake's emails. While I was crushed and eager to confront him, I decided not to so I could keep snooping. The guilt consumed me, but I couldn't stop checking his email and discovered more emails from Keisha with pictures and videos. I never said a word. I wanted to keep the peace and Blake to keep his passcode, so I'd know what he was doing.

Sometimes I wished I never began snooping because our relationship was great before I found out the truth. I was so hurt and torn. Other times, I wanted to kill myself so the pain would go away once and for all. Then I'd come to my senses. I knew I had to either leave Blake or stop snooping and love him for who he was. He was so different from anyone else I'd ever met. I loved him, but my love was conditional.

Every time we went out, Blake looked at women walking by and made remarks about how hot they were. In all fairness, most of the time, Blake was very loving toward me, even when I was being a bitch to him. He suffered from depression, which was hard for me to deal with. When he got depressed, I tried to stay positive, but I could only do so much. I couldn't save him.

After I snooped through Blake's messages, I became a better detective and started rummaging through his closet. The energy felt dark and secretive. I felt uncomfortable being there, but I looked through his drawers for clues that he was cheating. I found condoms in his shoe, pulled them out, and counted them, upset and unsure of what to do next. I wanted to leave him so badly, but the thought made me burst into tears. I wondered why I loved him so much. Was love supposed to hurt this badly? Did I deserve everything he was doing to me because of how I treated Lance? Maybe karma was real, and I deserved to go through all this pain. Tears rolled down my cheeks as I sat on the floor, trying to figure out what to do, feeling hurt and alone, and wishing I could talk to someone. When I finally calmed down, I decided not to tell him. It was best not to jump to conclusions. I took a few deep breaths and put the condoms back the way I found them.

Then Blake went out of town for the day on a work trip. At least, that's what he told me. He wasn't due back home until late that night, so I checked his condom supply, and two were missing. My heart sank and I lost it. I felt so stupid. I realized that he would never stop cheating on me. At least he was using condoms.

The next day, one of the condoms reappeared in the shoe. Now I had enough evidence to confront him. Just as I thought he would, Blake got angry at me for snooping in his closet. I kept asking who he had sex with, but he denied everything. He said I was crazy and he would never cheat on me. I threatened to break up with him if he didn't tell me, and finally, he said that the other condom was in his truck, so I demanded to see it. He threw me his keys and told me to find the condom myself. There were a bunch of condoms in the glove box, so I couldn't confirm my suspicions, but I did have a little peace of mind.

Blake complained that he was uncomfortable living in his own home because of my accusations. I felt terrible and promised I'd never snoop again, even though I knew I would. I couldn't help myself because I didn't trust him one bit. Blake wanted us to go to therapy, but I thought therapy was for losers. I was stubborn about it, convinced I was strong enough to get through anything without help. I wish I'd at least tried therapy. Over time, I built a huge wall around my heart so I wouldn't get hurt anymore. We were both happier that way. After all, I cheated on him every time I went to Vegas.

Despite the drama, Blake and I went to many festivals and parties, and there was never a dull moment. Blake was always the life of the party and attracted exciting people into our lives. I got into drugs more and more. They were everywhere. Guys walked around with baggies asking women if they wanted a bump. Sometimes I asked Blake if I could try whatever the guys were offering. Most of the time, he said no. That didn't stop me from pretending to go to the bathroom and finding the guy offering drugs so I could get a bump.

I hid the real me from Blake and only let him know a small part. While I let him control me, I also rebelled by doing things behind his back. Blake had no idea that I was buying and using drugs. Each time, I told myself it would be the last weekend that I used for a while. During the week, I beat myself up about it. I really wanted to quit, but I had no idea how to have fun without alcohol and drugs. I realized I'd never stop using if I continued this lifestyle.

Addiction is tough. I enjoyed feeling like I didn't have a care in the world, but often wondered why I couldn't just enjoy life as is. Why was I trying to escape? What about my life was so bad that I needed drugs? At first, I thought that I simply enjoyed not having a care in the world, but I also wondered if I used drugs to deal with something I'd never acknowledged, some underlying trauma that I shoved down. Maybe if I'd given therapy a chance, I could have made better choices. It wasn't until years later that I questioned why I chased sex and drugs and stayed in abusive relationships. Was it because I was so sheltered as a child and the forbidden became irresistible? Did I feel guilty about being with Kevin and betraying Christina? Had I ever blamed Kevin for taking advantage of me at a time when I needed safety and guidance? Or did I still blame myself?

Drugs made me feel confident and invincible. When I was high, I had inspiring visions of a blissful future. After I sobered up, I realized those visions gave me hope for my future, but I had to choose to make it amazing. I knew I had the option to change my life at any moment. The question was always, when would I be ready to change?

# CHAPTER FIFTEEN

Going to Cancun was another dream I had for a long time, but I always thought it was impossible unless I had some rich guy to take me there. After doing some research, I discovered it might be affordable. I suggested to Blake that we skip Burning Man in 2016 and instead go to Cancun. Blake seemed disappointed but eventually agreed.

On our first night in Cancun, we walked around and checked out all the bars and lounges at our hotel. The next day, we drove to Tulum, where we visited the ancient ruins and went to the beach. The ocean was breathtaking, with warm, blue water and calm, perfect waves. We sat by the water, where I drank the best Piña Coladas I'd ever tasted. Then we went to Playa Maya on a boat tour to see the ruins from the ocean. What a beautiful view! A boat took us to the coral reef, where I went snorkeling. Blake stayed aboard because he couldn't swim. As I jumped off the boat, I immediately panicked over the size of the waves until one of the crew jumped in the water to help me. He steadied me, pointed to hundreds of tiny fish swimming below, and then showed me how to put my face in the water and breathe through the snorkel. Once I got the hang of it, I swam alongside the fish, thinking how lucky I was. What an incredible experience, especially after I forgot how terrified I'd been just moments ago.

We spent the evening at a restaurant on the beach where we sat on swings, looking out at the sun setting over the sea. After dinner, a young man approached us and offered us a package deal for Daddy O's nightclub, where we could get a VIP table, unlimited drinks, and a free ride to the club. We decided to do it. When we arrived, a man greeted us and walked us past the endless line into the club to our VIP table, where they treated us like celebrities. The club quickly got packed, and when Blake went upstairs to the bathroom, he came back with a warning.

"Be careful," he said. "There's a guy standing outside the bathrooms selling coke. He's very persistent."

I laughed it off, but inside I was torn because I'd promised myself that I'd stay sober in Cancun. On my way to the bathroom, I planned to just say no if the guy approached me. Sure enough, he was there when I got to the top of the stairs. He put his finger under his nose and made a sniffing sound.

I said no, but he tried to follow me into the ladies' room. I stopped in the doorway. "I told you; I'm not interested."

Back at the table, I felt proud of myself for saying no and told Blake about it. We continued to drink until we both got tipsy, and I kept thinking about the cocaine. When I went to the bathroom again, I asked the dealer if he had a bag for twenty dollars, but he insisted the smallest amount he could sell me was sixty. I hesitated. I didn't need that much coke for a few days in Cancun, but he could see how much I wanted it. "Come here," he beckoned.

I followed him into a side room, where he asked me to show him my pussy and to touch his cock. "No way," I said and walked out. I decided to give him the money instead, and I did a little bump before walking back to our table.

"I was worried about you," Blake said.

"I'm fine," I assured him. I felt bad for being secretive, but I knew he wouldn't understand.

Eventually, we left our table to dance, and guys began circling me as soon as we stepped onto the dance floor. They didn't care that I was with Blake. They tried to touch me while I danced, and I moved closer to Blake. I felt like piranhas were attacking me, and Blake made me feel safe.

He went to the bathroom again while I waited at the bar for my change. A guy who worked at the club asked in broken English if I wanted to enter the bikini contest. "No, thank you," I told him.

He leaned in closer. "I'd personally appreciate it if you would, and you could win the grand prize: five hundred dollars."

That got my attention. "I'm waiting for my boyfriend, but I'll ask when he gets back."

Before Blake returned, I decided I wanted to enter. After all, he'd been complaining that he missed the spontaneous me. At first, Blake wasn't happy, but I reminded him we were in Cancun and that I'd probably never get this opportunity again. He said fine, as long as I was safe. When the man returned, I told him I'd enter the contest. He excitedly showed me to a door leading to a stairway.

"Follow me," he instructed. Blake was right behind me, and a second man followed Blake. We reached the top of the stairs and entered another door into the dressing room, but when I turned around, Blake was gone. "Oh no," I thought, it's a trap! What would they do now that we were separated? There were lots of women trying on bikinis, and a bald guy with a blue beard walked around like he was in charge. I asked him where they had taken my boyfriend. "Don't worry," he tried to reassure me. "He's fine. Just relax and get ready for the contest.

Panicked, I walked out to find Blake. What had I done now? Alcohol, drugs, and Naomi are not a good combination. I knew Blake was worried about the contest. I walked around the club trying to find him, imagining they put a bag over his head and took him somewhere to keep as a hostage. I wondered how I'd live with myself if they hurt him, or even worse, killed him. All this trouble was because I wanted to be in a silly bikini contest. The man who'd asked me to enter the contest saw me. "Are you okay?" he asked.

"I'm looking for my boyfriend," I said. "Do you know where he is?"

"Yes, I put him in the VIP section so he could see you better." He led me to where Blake was sitting, promising that everything was fine.

Hugging Blake, I told him how concerned I was when I couldn't find him. He said he was worried too, but I assured him I'd be okay.

Back upstairs, the bearded man handed me a beautiful sky-blue bikini, and after changing, I sat on a couch next to the other contestants. They were so young, and although I felt insecure, I reminded myself that I was beautiful, too. Then I remembered why I was doing the contest — to have fun and be spontaneous.

The crowd went wild, clapping and screaming as I strutted onto the stage. I did a little dance and then joined the other women. Even though I didn't win, it was an amazing experience. I got dressed and went back to Blake, who looked unhappy.

"Everyone likes you and talks to you while I sit by myself," Blake sulked.

The following night, we went to another club where the performers wore black tape over their breasts and naughty bits. Each hour, the dancers performed two and three at a time on a tall stripper pole. I kept telling Blake I wanted to dance on the pole, and he encouraged me to go for it, so I asked a manager if I could do some pole tricks, and he said yes. They had no idea what I was about to do. The dancers left the stage, and I had it all to myself. I climbed to the top and posed, enjoying the moment. Everyone crowded around, clapping as the spotlight followed my every move and I made my way down the pole doing tricks and flips. Security guards escorted me off the stage when I got to the bottom. They handed me a dozen roses, praised me for the amazing performance, but told me that I was a liability to the club if I got injured. I politely thanked them, basking in my moment of glory. Blake congratulated me for being spontaneous, and the crowd gathered around, telling me how much they loved my performance. Before we left Cancun, Blake thanked me for insisting on the change of plans. It wasn't comparable to Burning Man, but he had an amazing time.

Blake's house was decorated like a nightclub complete with a DJ booth, purple walls, dark blue ceilings, and a stripper pole in the middle of the living room. We built a sectional couch in purple and dark blue faux fur to match the walls and ceiling. Every year, we had several big parties, each with a different theme and DJ lineup. People from all walks of life showed up, and the house would swell with old friends and new people I'd never met. Sometimes the parties lasted for two days.

People felt free at our parties because there was no judgment. We just wanted everyone to have a great time. I loved dancing and performing on the pole, especially after I was fueled up from a few drinks and whatever drugs I'd taken. I felt invincible and went wild when the crowd cheered, loving the attention. I also taught other people how to do pole tricks.

We started going to swinger sex parties, and at first, I was uncomfortable because I worried that Blake would have sex with other women. I didn't mind oral sex if I felt included, but it often seemed like Blake didn't know how to have a fair threesome because he showered whoever was joining us with all the attention. I felt ignored and excluded, then sad and angry. There was no pleasure in it for me. I thought all the other women were lucky because he gave them oral, which I so badly desired. I asked why he gave other women that pleasure and not me, and he said since I wouldn't allow him to have intercourse with them, that was his only option.

Life seemed so unfair in the sexual world. I was afraid Blake would leave me if I didn't allow him to do these things, yet I couldn't bear the thought of him having sex with someone else. All I could think of was how tainted my relationship with Lance got after I allowed him to have sex with whoever he wanted. I feared the same thing would happen if Blake had intercourse with someone else. I questioned whether I was selfish by not letting him do what he wanted. Maybe I was too controlling, and that made him lust after other women even more. Each time we had threesomes, one of us always felt left out, and we often ended up arguing.

I enjoyed flirting with women, which was as far as I wanted to take it. Still, before I knew it, Blake said he wanted to explore polyamory. I told him that I wasn't into it. He didn't reply but I know he heard me.

The more I allowed him to play around, the more he wanted. I thought if I had sex with him more often that maybe he could be faithful, but I was wrong.

Building a massive wall around my heart was the only way I knew how to protect myself, which made it hard for us to communicate. Trust and communication are key to any successful relationship, and we didn't have much of either. I don't know how I survived all those parties. I'm sad to say this, but when I did drugs, nothing bothered me. The after-parties sometimes turned into sex parties, and drugs helped me cope with them. I tried to block it out until I became numb.

I wasn't a fan of orgies, but Blake usually had his eye on one or two women from the party. I was so uncomfortable unless I was on drugs. Then I didn't mind as much.

"Fine," I'd say. "Have sex with them."

He'd insist that the other woman he picked up should sleep in our bed so they could cuddle, which meant she slept between us. I rarely allowed this, but I got tired of hearing him complain about my selfishness. I felt like crawling under a rock and never coming out. Sometimes I cried myself to sleep.

Our friend, Logan, showed up to our parties with homemade sex toys: dildos motorized by power tools, an electric sex wand, floggers, butt plugs, gags, whips, chains, handcuffs, blindfolds, and other goodies. He also had a contraption called "fire and ice," made of candle wax and ice cubes. The melted candle wax and ice droplets created a hot and cold sensation on the skin. Logan would set his bag of toys on the floor inside the back door and take off his leather pants, leaving him completely naked. After greeting everyone, he'd set out lines of cocaine, and that's when our parties turned kinky. Some people left as soon as he showed up, knowing that our casual dance party was about to end.

Blake and I often had sex in front of other people at our parties. I loved having an audience, and people loved watching us have sex. It seemed everyone had heard about Blake's big cock and wanted to see it. I got high from the excitement and felt like a porn star.

Our next-door neighbors were like-minded, hosting swinger parties at their house. The owner was a middle-aged man with a girlfriend in her late twenties. The parties were "invite only," and consent was a big deal; if someone was unruly or violated any of the house rules, they weren't invited back.

Their bedroom was a sexual playground with something for everyone. There was an open coffin, a bed built over a cage, and a bondage wheel on the wall. A sex swing hung from the ceiling alongside an old-fashioned OBGYN table, a dental chair, a spinning stripper pole, homemade sex machines, and an array of dildos. Usually, there was an orgy going on in the bed. Some people got tied to the BDSM bondage wheel and flogged, and others wore leashes as they crawled on their hands and knees, pretending to be animals. A heated pool and steam sauna provided the perfect break from the sexual Olympics happening inside the house.

Blake's thirst for sexual adventure intensified, and his requests grew bolder. One night, he invited a friend named Jayden to come over to drink and DJ with us. After dinner, Blake asked Jayden to have sex with me. I interrupted him. I didn't want to have sex with his friend, and Jayden agreed. He didn't want to have sex with me, either. But Blake insisted. "You split from your wife, and you know you want to get laid."

Jayden doubled down. "I don't want to hook up with your girlfriend."

"It's okay," Blake insisted. "I want you to have sex with my sexy girlfriend."

I had Blake figured out. He was persistent, even retrieving condoms from the bedroom, and eventually, we caved. I stood and faced them, side by side on the sofa, kneeling in front of Blake first. I teased the tip of his cock with my tongue and watched as Jayden's began to bulge and twitch beneath his jeans. As I took Blake's huge cock as far as I could into my mouth, I freed Jayden's now rock-hard erection and began to stroke it. They laughed and joked about how it looked like I was skiing because I had a penis in each hand. Blake wanted me on top, so I climbed onto Jayden's lap and rode him while I kept Blake hard with my hand. Then I went down on Jayden again. I thought if I could get him to orgasm, then it would all be over, but Blake wasn't satisfied, and he insisted that I ride Jayden some more.

I sat backward on Jayden the second time because I didn't want to look at his face. Finally, I'd had enough. All I could think about was that Blake would use this as an excuse to have sex with another woman. I couldn't believe I'd fallen for his manipulation again. I stopped and told them it was hurting, and I was done. Then I went and got cleaned up, trying to hide how upset I was.

Blake and I had sex again before we went to sleep. He was so turned on, and I played along. "Maybe I needed to do this more often," I thought. "Maybe we could have an even more intense sex life if I had sex with other guys." But I wasn't into screwing random guys for free. I loved Blake and only wanted him. Just as I predicted, he said that because I had sex with another guy, it justified him being with another woman. I couldn't believe I'd let myself get into that situation. "This is so unfair because I didn't even want to have sex with your friend," I said.

"But you did."

"I know, but only because you wanted me to," I cried.

I wished I could turn back time and have a do-over, still believing that maybe if I accepted his demands and kept my mouth shut, we might have a decent relationship. I didn't understand why I was so jealous and controlling. Why couldn't I just let Blake be who he was? Why did I get so hurt and upset? Maybe it was because we were raised differently. I'd never heard of anyone openly having more than one partner until I dated Lance. I wasn't even sure I wanted to understand it, but I knew I wanted to be open to the ways of this world that sometimes still felt so foreign to me. For all I knew, this was normal, and I was the one who was naïve and stubborn.

Little did I know that my entire life was about to change.

# CHAPTER SIXTEEN

At the beginning of 2017, I started thinking about having a baby. Throughout my twenties, I was convinced that I should avoid having kids because Kevin warned me it would destroy my body, and I needed my body to make money. A decade later, I realized Kevin had taken advantage of my desperation to run away from the Amish. He didn't know everything—and maybe I did want kids, regardless of what would happen to my body during pregnancy. Lance had made it clear that he didn't want more kids because he already had a daughter who wasn't part of his life. Now that I was with Blake, I really wanted to have a family and felt like time was running out. But he kept saying he wasn't ready to abandon his party lifestyle. Finally, he agreed that we could start trying for a baby after one last blowout at the Burning Man festival in August.

In February, we were celebrating a friend's birthday with a campout in the desert when I met Blake's co-worker, Waylen. At first, I thought he was a cop as his truck roared into the camp, headlights blazing. When Waylen first jumped out of the truck, I thought he was funny looking. He was average height with dark, wild curly hair and glasses. Blake introduced us. Immediately I knew he wasn't like Blake's other friends. Waylen's respectful demeanor made me feel unusually shy, but I liked his bashful smile and mad scientist vibe, and I changed my mind about his looks. He wasn't funny-looking; he was unique.

We made eye contact, and Waylen asked if we had an air pump, explaining that his air pressure was low because he'd deflated his tires when he got stuck in the sand on the way over. I didn't understand why he'd deflate his tires, but I went and got the pump, and we headed toward his truck. As he walked, Waylen kept his hands clasped behind his back and looked straight ahead with a smirk. I wondered what he was thinking with an expression like that. I tried to figure out his nationality, but I had no idea. Waylen smiled and said, "This isn't going to do much but it's better than nothing."

"Why did you deflate your tires when you got stuck?" I asked.

"The tires are more grippy with less air," he explained.

We were only alone for a few minutes, but I felt disappointed when his tires were full and we had to return to the party.

Our parties got so crazy. I wondered why Blake would risk exposing his private life to a co-worker. I felt awkward letting loose because I didn't want Blake to get in trouble.

At some point, I got bored and decided to go off by myself on a go-kart ride. A few minutes in, the engine got stuck in fast mode. I forgot there were no brakes! The go-kart stalled on a hill, and when I restarted it, the front end reared up, almost landing on top of me. I could barely hold on before it took off again, reminding me of a young horse, not yet buggy trained, rearing up and running off. I came barreling back into the camp, screaming at everyone to move out of the way. Luckily, the go-kart stopped abruptly. Shaken, I explained what happened, but no one seemed interested except Waylen, who asked if he could look at it for me. I told him he could and went to get a drink to calm down. Waylen got tools from his truck and went to work on the go-kart. Then he took it for a spin, and I watched him steer skillfully across the dunes.

When Waylen resumed working on the go-kart, I walked over to see what he was doing, and he stood up and wiped his brow. "I'm wiring a switch to the motor so you can just flip it to shut it off."

"Wow," I thought, "this guy must be a genius." We continued to talk while he fixed a few other electrical things around the camp. When my friend, Marissa, and I took our tops off as we usually did, I suddenly felt uncomfortable because Waylen was there. I felt shy, but I could tell Waylen didn't care, so I decided not to think about it, to be myself and have a great time. Marissa and I were being wild. While we danced, she dropped to her knees, peeled my panties aside, and ran her tongue down my pussy. The party went wild. Everyone was used to us being naughty and promiscuous. Waylen looked like he was having a great time. I kept wondering about him. Was he open-minded, or was it all an act? Nothing seemed to faze him, and he was sweet and polite to everyone.

After the weekend ended, I didn't think much about Waylen except to ask Blake if everything was okay between them at work. Blake assured me it was and asked why I was so concerned about Waylen. "I just don't want things to be awkward for you at work," I said.

"Everything's great," he insisted. "Waylen and I are cool."

Waylen came over the following week to help Blake fix his truck. There was nothing Waylen couldn't fix, and I was happy that Blake finally had a guy friend. I made them tea and sandwiches and kept offering them more to eat. We both enjoyed having Waylen around. Blake even started inviting him to the clubs with us. We adopted him into our world. Waylen was like the brother I always wanted since leaving the Amish — someone I could talk to about anything without sexual tension.

On the Fourth of July, Blake and I went to a large party on the beach near Venice and invited Waylen. Blake was trying to be nice to me, but I was tired of him running off and flirting with other women. It bothered me less this time because I was hanging out with Waylen, who stayed with me when Blake ran off to flirt. I told Waylen I was going to break up with Blake.

"But Blake loves you," Waylen said.

"Yeah, right," I sighed. "He doesn't even bother to hang out with me."

Waylen shook his head. "Don't break up with Blake; he does love you."

I watched Blake dancing with another woman as if I didn't exist. "How can you justify that when he's right there flirting with someone else?"

188

Waylen defended his friend. "Blake's just different."

It was almost dark when Waylen and I left our beach blanket to go pee. We started heading back, only to realize we had no idea where our blanket and belongings were. Blake was nowhere to be found either. My phone was with the blanket and Waylen's phone was dead, so we couldn't call him. Finally, I found someone we knew who led us back to our stuff. It was already dark, and we were still looking for Blake.

Suddenly, we heard sirens and saw police lights racing down the beach. I thought maybe someone got hurt, but a passerby said the cops were coming to shut down the party, and they did. An officer walked up to Waylen and asked him to dispose of his beer. Waylen asked how, and she repeated, "Get rid of it!" Waylen dumped it on the beach in front of her and she let us go. I kept calling Blake until he answered, and we could finally go home.

When Blake was asked to DJ for a birthday party in an old porn studio, we invited Waylen and our friend, Grace. Each room of the studio had a different theme. The ball pit grossed me out because so many half-naked sweaty people were going in and out. Grace and I did cocaine and had a great time dancing. Blake DJ'd until he got drunk and started chasing other women, so Waylen and I took over. Blake had brought a fucking robot that came with a ten-inch dildo attached. The robot's head was an old toaster, the arms were wood, and the body was made from metal scrap with pink Barbie hot wheel tires. The dildo attached to the glides of a drawer, connected to a battery that powered the dildo and gave it the back-and-forth sex motion. The dildo was the perfect height for doggy style. When Blake came back to DJ, Waylen and I decided to take the fucking robot for a ride.

Waylen was painfully shy, so I thought maybe I could help him find a woman who'd use the robot with him. As we passed women at the party, we held up condoms and asked if they wanted to have sex with the fucking robot. But they seemed scared; some were offended. Sadly, no one wanted to have sex with the fucking robot.

Blake liked to fuck me with the robot in front of an audience. I felt like a queen because I was the center of attention.

Before long, Waylen was at our house every weekend and came along to all the parties. Blake had his birthday party at a swingers' club in a private home that year. He wanted a threesome with another woman, but I wasn't in the mood. We got in the pool naked and encouraged Waylen to get in, too. Waylen was so cute, insisting he was too scared because there were so many naked people in the pool already. He stood on the pool's edge debating whether to get in. I promised him it would be a memory he wouldn't forget, but I secretly hoped he would get in naked because maybe I could get a peek at his penis. I'd never thought of him that way, but I was curious. Out of nowhere, he jumped in, somehow removing his underwear mid-air. I felt a little awkward being naked around him, but I got the peek I was looking for and became even more intrigued when I saw its potential. The three of us giggled and splashed in the pool.

I was fed up with Blake and his shenanigans and felt ready to break up with him. It was all I could think about, but I didn't know how or when to do it. I'd become numb to his comments about all the hot women he wanted to screw. Meanwhile, Waylen and I sat on the sidelines, talking about our families, work, and everything we wanted out of life. Waylen's dream was to live in the woods with room to tinker on fifty trucks. As he described it, I got a funny feeling in my stomach. It wasn't quite butterflies. It felt like an awakening of possibilities of things I hadn't yet dreamed or imagined.

Waylen had always felt like a brother or the best friend I'd always wished for. With Waylen, I could be honest and tell him anything and feel safe from judgment. I'd never thought of him sexually, and it wasn't worth the risk of losing my new best friend.

One night after dinner at our house, Blake casually asked Waylen, "You want to have sex with my girlfriend tonight?"

Waylen looked uncomfortable. "No way," he said.

Blake kept pushing. "Come on, Naomi, have sex with Waylen."

"No way," I echoed. "Waylen's like a brother to me."

Part of me didn't believe what I was saying, but I was so sick of Blake and his demands, and I wouldn't let him be the puppet master again. Not with Waylen. "No way in hell am I having sex with Waylen," I repeated. "No offense to Waylen."

To satisfy Blake, I gave him a blow job right there on the couch in front of Waylen, but even so, Blake kept insisting, and I kept ignoring his request. "Just finger her then," he suggested.

Waylen looked at me, and I saw the desire in his eyes. His expression melted my defenses. I caved, spreading my knees and arching my back, a silent invitation. I continued sucking Blake's cock while Waylen knelt in front of the couch and pushed up my skirt. The warmth of his hands on my backside made me gasp. He slid his finger inside me, and I squeezed down on it, instantly wanting more. At first, I felt awkward trying to finish Blake while Waylen and I were having our first sexual encounter. I was surprised at how skilled Waylen was with his fingers. He got me dripping wet, and I was enjoying myself. Blake stood up and unzipped Waylen's pants, encouraging him to go further. Waylen was so cute and shy. He sat on the couch smiling, and I could tell he was nervous. Blake wanted me to ride Waylen backward, and I was relieved I didn't have to look at Waylen while I rode him. It was too weird. His cock felt so good inside me. Not too big, not too small. He was just right.

Blake sat on the floor, trying to stroke himself back into an erection. I got on all fours so I to help him orally while Waylen fucked me from behind. I couldn't help but laugh, which was hard with Blake's cock in my mouth. I was having a great time with Waylen. He was making me feel some kind of way. He kept giving me orgasms.

Blake realized how much I was enjoying Waylen, and he suddenly lost interest and went to mope on the couch by himself. I could tell he regretted encouraging us in the first place. It was hard to ignore his dramatic sulking, and Waylen slowed his pace. I wanted to keep fucking Waylen, but not like this.

"Can we stop now?" I asked Blake.

"Whatever," Blake said.

Waylen pulled out, and we separated. Then Blake and I went to bed while Waylen slept on the couch.

Blake didn't talk to me much until Wednesday after he got home from work. During dinner, he brought it up.

"I told you I didn't want to have sex with him," I argued.

Blake looked disturbed. "But you did."

"Seriously, I can't believe you just said that. Once again, you practically forced me to have sex with your friend and blamed me afterward. It's just another setup." I could feel the anger tingling from my brain into my body, and I felt like I was going to explode.

"You were the one who unzipped Waylen's pants, not me," I reminded him.

"That doesn't mean you had to have sex with him."

Shaking my head in disbelief, I decided to take the blame and agree so we could quit fighting.

Blake wouldn't let it go. "I could tell you liked it too much. Do you want to have sex with him again?"

"No, I don't." I changed the subject. "How are things with Waylen at work?"

"Fine," he said.

Everything changed after that weekend. Blake seemed worried and didn't talk much. I couldn't stop thinking about Waylen, and I wondered if he thought about me or felt like I did. The days and weeks seemed endless. Out of respect for Blake, I didn't contact Waylen. I considered the possibility that I was delusional and making up this incredible dynamic I felt with Waylen. Maybe sex with him really wasn't that great. But I didn't really believe that I imagined those feelings. I thought if I could just have sex with Waylen one more time, I could be sure. I needed confirmation that I was attracted to him, but I knew I loved how he made me feel. If only I could talk to him.

I waited three weeks before asking Blake if he and Waylen had plans for the weekend, and quickly, Blake accused me of wanting to have sex with Waylen again. I assured him that I didn't. But Blake sneered. "Yeah, right."

Now I longed to talk to Waylen. I knew he was living in his big military truck, which he called the Dragonwagon, in the parking lot where they worked. Blake told me Waylen was working long hours and probably wouldn't be able to get away for a while. I told him Waylen was probably overworked and needed a break. "We should invite him to the beach party on Sunday." I mentioned it several times and could tell he was getting annoyed, but on Saturday, Blake confirmed we could go to the beach party. I felt like jumping up and down with joy as I messaged Waylen. That night, I felt like a kid waiting for Christmas to come.

When I heard Waylen's truck pull in the next morning, I jumped out of bed.

"Why is Waylen here?" Blake asked.

"I told him to meet us here for the beach party."

Blake banged his fist on the wall. "Why didn't you consult with me before you invited him?"

I remained calm, too excited to see Waylen to be bothered. "I asked you a few times last night," I explained. "I thought you knew that I invited him. Maybe you weren't listening."

At first, I tried to ignore Waylen, for Blake's sake. Once at the party, Blake got drunk and danced with everyone but me, and I eventually got the nerve to ask Waylen if he thought much about the last time we saw each other. Waylen's face turned red, and he said he didn't know what I was talking about then changed the subject, so we started talking about Las Vegas. "I know what you do for work when you're there," Waylen said.

I didn't feel the need to lie to him. Feeling empowered, I admitted that I saw clients outside the club.

"I already know that, too."

"How?" I asked.

"Most exotic dancers have some clients on the side."

I felt relieved that I could finally be honest with someone.

"I tried to tell Blake," Waylen said. "But he's in denial."

"Please don't tell him I told you," I begged.

"Don't worry, I won't."

"Does it upset you?" I asked.

Waylen shrugged. "No. I think it's cool that you're brave enough to do that."

"So how do you really feel about our three-way party?"

Waylen walked away laughing. "I don't know what you're talking about."

Then he turned and faced me again. "I loved it, but I don't want to be a homewrecker."

"You wouldn't be a homewrecker," I assured him.

Waylen took a step backward, ending the conversation. "We shouldn't talk about this while Blake is close by."

I gave in, and we continued to party.

After that, Waylen and I messaged each other on Facebook until Blake found out and asked Waylen not to message me anymore. Then Waylen and I were just more careful about not getting caught. The urge to be together intensified each day. Waylen was on my mind every second, and I felt like a teenager with a waterfall between my legs because I was so wet and tingly all the time. It had been a long time since I'd felt that way. He wasn't my type, but I was attracted to his personality. I tried to ignore my feelings, but I wanted to have sex with Waylen again and not feel like I was cheating on Blake. So, I decided Blake could have sex with our friend Grace. She was like a sister to me, and I trusted her. The next weekend, I asked Blake if Waylen could come with us to an outdoor concert. He didn't say no, but I could tell he wasn't excited about it either. I desperately wanted to see Waylen, so I had to devise a great plan.

I told Blake that I really wanted Grace to come over so he could fulfill his fantasies with her, and he immediately got flushed. "Are you serious?"

"Yes, it's only fair since I had sex with Waylen." I didn't know how to contain my excitement, but I had to keep my plan a secret.

I wore a short, sexy, red dress over lace, thong underwear, and when Waylen and Grace showed up, I made drinks for everyone. Waylen looked so hot in his little shorts, and I kept glancing at them, recalling what was under them with anticipation. Blake and Grace went out to the backyard, and Waylen stayed in the kitchen. He asked me if his shorts were okay, and I told him he looked great in them, but he said he was embarrassed. "Why?" I asked.

He just laughed, too shy to tell me. I took a closer look and discovered his secret—a big boner his shorts couldn't hide. I just laughed. Before that moment, I didn't know if he liked me as much as I liked him.

The concert was close enough to take Blake's go-kart and Waylen's electric drift trike that had one seat with a big battery behind it. Grace didn't want to sit on the battery, so I offered to ride with Waylen, and she was happy to ride with Blake. I was beyond excited to ride to the concert with Waylen. I held him tightly, reaching around his waist and grabbing his big boner. He returned the favor, reaching back with one hand and fingering my soaking-wet vagina. We had a blast together at the concert.

After we got home, Blake started up the sound system, and while Waylen DJ'd, I encouraged Blake and Grace to go for it. Once they started undressing each other, I motioned to Waylen, who ran to his truck to get a condom. I stripped naked and sat on the couch, anxiously waiting and playing with my clit, sliding a finger inside. Waylen returned, grinning. "I see you're ready for me."

"Always," I whispered and unzipped his pants. He knelt in front of the couch. Wrapping my legs around his waist, I pulled him close as his shaft slid inside me. I wanted to kiss him so badly, but Blake was on the sofa next to us with Grace. Even so, our souls felt so connected that I momentarily forgot. Each thrust went deeper than the one before and waves of pulsating pleasure rippled through my body. Waylen gazed into my eyes with pure passion as his hands gripped my hips. I could tell he wanted to let go but couldn't because Blake was right there.

Blake and Grace were done before us and sat there watching. Blake looked crushed. "Do you want us to stop?" I asked.

Blake shook his head and said, "Whatever."

There was a moment of awkward silence. I felt bad for Blake and had no idea what to say. Standing up, I made more drinks for everyone, which lightened the mood. Blake continued to DJ, and we all danced before Grace announced that she was tired and ready to go home. Blake wanted Waylen to drive her home, but I insisted Waylen was too drunk.

"You just don't want Waylen to leave," Blake said.

"No," I assured him. "He drank too much to drive."

Waylen quickly offered to pay for Grace's Uber, and the three of us stayed up and listened to music before going to bed. Waylen slept on the couch while Blake and I went to our bedroom. Of course, Blake wanted more sex before we went to sleep. Either he was turned on because he'd just been with Grace, or he was trying to prove himself to me because I'd been with Waylen again.

Blake was in a bad mood the next morning, complaining that I did whatever I wanted without asking him first. I was starting to see that his demands were hypocritical and ridiculous, but I apologized to keep the peace. Being submissive took less energy than arguing.

Waylen was on my mind day and night. I wanted to see him again, but Blake knew something was up and stopped inviting him over. Finally, I came up with a scheme to see Waylen. The Chamber of Commerce held a meeting right near where Waylen worked, so I decided to go to the meeting with the excuse that I could find some potential prospects for the network marketing company I worked for. Then I asked Waylen if we could meet up afterward. He was hesitant. "Does Blake know?

"Blake doesn't need to know," I said.

Waylen sighed heavily. "I'll feel bad if we cheat on Blake."

"Don't worry about Blake. He's cheated on me many times."

"Two wrongs don't make a right."

I persisted, longing to be in his arms, and he agreed to see me that night. I went to the Chamber of Commerce meeting and snapped a few pictures to prove to Blake I was there, then Waylen picked me up in his big Rock Crawler. I could tell he was nervous, but I was nervous, too. I felt guilty, but seeing Waylen was all I'd thought about. He took me to eat, and then we went back to his place — the Dragonwagon in the parking lot. I curled up in the front seat to ensure no one would see me as we pulled in. The passion between us was intense, and we made love to each other for over an hour. Time went by quickly, and I didn't want to leave. Blake texted, asking when I'd be home. I bought myself some more time by telling him I went to dinner with a girlfriend from the

196

Chamber meeting. He didn't question me after that.

I wondered how I could be lucky enough to meet such a loving, caring, and unique soul like Waylen. I never wanted to wake up from this dream. My heart was radiant and joyful, and I couldn't contain my newfound love and excitement.

When I got home, I tried to act normal. Blake was working in the garage. I said hi to him and went inside, then went to bed feeling more torn than ever. The thought of breaking up with Blake was unbearable and I couldn't think of a solution where everyone would end up happy. But I knew there was no turning back.

# CHAPTER SEVENTEEN

Everything felt so right with Waylen, and I began thinking that maybe I was fated to be with Waylen instead of with Blake. But if I broke up with Blake to be with Waylen, Blake would hate both of us. I figured the best thing to do was to keep seeing Waylen and not tell Blake. Maybe the excitement would wear off, and my feelings for Waylen would fade.

A week after Waylen and I hooked up, I told Blake I was going to my salsa and hip-hop dance class. Instead, I went to see Waylen, who suggested we go for a walk in the park. He was acting weird and didn't want to make love to me. We sat in my car in the empty parking lot. "What's wrong?" I asked.

Waylen wrung his hands. "I feel bad for Blake and don't want to be a homewrecker like my ex-girlfriend's coworker who ruined my first relationship."

"You're not being a homewrecker, and Blake will never know."

"We should tell Blake," Waylen said.

I put my hands over his, trying to calm him. "Please don't tell him. We can stop seeing each other for now, but we can't tell him. He'll be so hurt."

I felt so confused. As much as I wanted Waylen, I still wasn't ready to have that conversation with Blake. Waylen and I failed to come up with a solution, but we ended up making love in the back seat. On my way home, I felt relieved that I didn't have to break up with Blake just yet. However, the next morning, our messages continued as usual. I was confused but happy. Waylen still liked me.

When I went to Vegas for work again, I messaged Waylen on Facebook to ask for his number, and we spent hours talking on the phone. From then on, it was difficult to focus on work because I always longed to be with Waylen. If nothing else, I decided never to start another relationship if I couldn't be myself and honest about who I was.

I left on Saturday instead of Sunday as originally planned, but I didn't tell Blake. On my way back, I stopped in Mojave to see a client, then spent the night with Waylen. We had a romantic evening making love. Cuddling and sleeping in Waylen's arms felt perfect. It was nice to feel loved and alive again. I had no idea where my relationship with Waylen was going, but I decided to ride the happy wave while it lasted.

Blake and I hosted a party for my twentieth anniversary away from the Amish, and a lot of our friends showed up to celebrate my freedom with me. I couldn't believe twenty years had slipped by—and had passed in the blink of an eye. It felt like yesterday that I left my family and everything familiar to me, I lived an amazing and crazy life and overcame many obstacles and challenges. I felt grateful for each experience — the good, the bad, and the crazy. Tears rolled down my cheeks, some sad, but most were happy. The greatest hardship I faced was not being with my family. I missed them dearly each and every day. I didn't get to see my little brothers and sisters grow up. I didn't know them well. It still made me uneasy when they asked about my life because I didn't like lying to them, but I was afraid they'd reject me if they knew who I was. Not having them in my life all those years hurt more than words can describe.

Rocking in a chair by the garage, I brushed my tears away. I promised myself that over the next twenty years, I'd be strong and take control of my life. That meant no more boyfriends who abused me in any way, or drugs to numb my pain. I wanted to live a clean and healthy lifestyle. I made a commitment to live the life I wanted to live instead of how other people wanted me to live. Feeling confident, I got up and went back to the party. Blake spotted me and grabbed my arm.

"Where were you?" he asked.

"Outside," I told him. "Reflecting on the last twenty years of my life."

"Welcome back," he said.

A group of porn stars was getting frisky in the kitchen, one of whom was famous for making women squirt. She made my friend squirt all over the kitchen floor. I could hardly believe my eyes. We had to get towels to clean up the mess. A large audience had gathered to watch. She looked at me. "You're next."

"Me?" I mouthed.

She nodded. "I'm ready to make you squirt."

The crowd nudged me forward. "Yeah, right," I thought. "It takes a lot to make me squirt." I dropped my panties and leaned against the kitchen counter, and she dropped to her knees and ate me out in front of the audience. Before I had time to think about it, she made me squirt what felt like gallons of liquid all over the floor. The audience laughed and clapped for us. Afterward, I danced on the pole until I was exhausted. Then I collapsed on a sofa, determined to sit and relax for a bit, but the lesbian porn star had different plans for me and asked if she could use her strap-on with me. The big, sky-blue strap-on dildo made me a little nervous, and I worried it would hurt, but she said she knew what she was doing. Once again, an audience gathered around us as she suited up into her pretty strap-on. She told me to get on the couch, then dropped to her knees and dominated me as no one had before. I was in a daze, dehydrated from squirting for the second time that night. She said she wanted to make me squirt again, but I was done. I'd had enough.

I ran to find Waylen to show him the big wet spot before I cleaned it up and found him in the kitchen. But when I described the scene in the living room, he brushed me off and said he didn't care to see it. He ignored me when I tried to hang out with him after that. I was so confused. I finally got him to talk to me, and he told me he was jealous. I was shocked. We weren't in a relationship; I was still Blake's girlfriend.

That was a red flag for me. However, I put myself in his shoes and felt bad for hurting his feelings, so I apologized, and we made up.

I was truly sick of Blake. Waylen and I sat on the couch discussing a possible future together while Blake had sex with the other porn star in our bed.

"What's wrong?" I asked.

"I don't like taking drugs," Waylen answered. "I don't feel good."

I got him some water and assured him he'd be okay because I'd only given him a small amount of molly.

Waylen swallowed the water down and rubbed his eyes. "I never want to do drugs ever again. You should stop, too; it can't be good for your brain."

I knew that was a promise I couldn't keep, but I agreed not to do any more that night.

Waylen looked at me and took my hand. "We have to tell Blake that we're having an affair."

Clearly, he couldn't handle drugs. I squeezed him back and politely asked him not to tell Blake, but he insisted.

"When do you plan on telling him?" I asked.

"As soon as he's done having sex with the porn star."

"Please wait, at least until tomorrow," I begged him. "Don't ruin my party."

Our friends were still dancing and having fun. I didn't want to air my dirty laundry in front of them; it was none of their business. It seemed that Waylen wanted revenge because I had squirted with the lesbian porn star. Blake and the porn star came out of the bedroom grinning, and I asked Blake if he enjoyed having sex with her. He said he had a great time. Waylen shook his head. "We have to tell him."

"Not now," I whispered.

Blake looked at us suspiciously. "What are you whispering about?"

Waylen blurted it out. "We're having an affair."

I couldn't believe it. A wave of heat rushed over every inch of my body, and I voiced the truth without thinking. "Yep," I said. "It's true, Blake. We cheated on you."

Blake took a step back. "No way. "I don't believe you."

"I'm really sorry, Blake."

"I'm sorry, too," Waylen said. "It's true; we cheated on you."

Blake was quiet for a moment. "I knew it." He threw an open palm that stopped short of hitting Waylen in the face. "We are done."

Everything got awkward, and most of our friends left. Blake grabbed my hand. "I can't believe you would do this to me after everything I've done for you!"

I apologized repeatedly. Blake said I could make it up to him by joining him and the porn star in our bedroom, and out of guilt, I said yes. He had me lay on my back while the porn star got on her hands and knees, straddling me while he had sex with her from behind. As I watched them together, I felt dead inside. I'd made some horrible choices and couldn't see any solution. My life was in total shambles. On top of everything, I was drunk and high.

After sex, Blake tried to cuddle both of us. I excused myself, went to check on Waylen, and found him wrapped in a blanket in the music room. "Are you okay?" I asked.

"Not really," he mumbled.

"Please sober up before you drive home," I said. "We'll figure this out."

"Let's leave and get a hotel room," he pleaded.

"I can't go tonight. I need to stay and figure things out with Blake."

I went back to the bedroom where Blake was cuddling with the porn star. "Could we have some alone time, please?" I asked.

The porn star got dressed and left. Blake sat up and rubbed his eyes. "What's your plan?" he asked.

"I plan on moving out," I replied.

He slumped over and put his head in his hands. "Please stay so we can work on our relationship."

I stared at him until he looked up at me. "Really, Blake? You want to work on our relationship now?"

"Yes," he insisted.

"Well, it's too late. We've tried to fix our relationship many times, and nothing's changed. If anything, we grow apart further each time. I'm over it. We're beyond fixable." We both cried as we talked.

"I don't know how I'll live without you," Blake sobbed. "You're my everything."

Keeping my arms crossed, I looked out the window. "You have a funny way of showing me that I'm your everything."

I stood at a crossroads. The unknown felt so scary. I was leaving Blake to be with Waylen even though I was unsure if it was the right path. Thankfully, the next day I was leaving to visit my family for two weeks. I told Blake that I would pack up and leave when I returned. He said he hoped I'd change my mind while I was gone.

Waylen quit his job, moved back to Phoenix, and asked me to join him. After I got back from visiting my family, I packed all my belongings and got rid of everything that no longer served me.

Saying goodbye to Blake was one of the hardest moments in my life. I couldn't believe it was actually happening. I imagined that we'd be together for eternity. We cried as we hugged each other goodbye. As I drove away, part of me wanted to turn back around, but I was determined to stick with my decision and start a new life. If I didn't like this new path, I could always give Blake another chance. I didn't understand why leaving him hurt so badly. It was the hardest thing I'd done besides leaving my family.

I moved to Phoenix to be with Waylen. I didn't have many belongings anymore, and Waylen arranged for me to stay in his mom's guest room until we found a place. The idea of meeting his family made me nervous. He'd told his mom, Shelly, and sister, Michelle, what I did for a living. Michelle freaked out because I was a stripper. She didn't want to meet me.

Shelly lived in a ritzy neighborhood called Scottsdale in a huge house, its interiors accented with silk flowers on the tables. She decorated the walls with paintings of Catholic saints, Mary and Joseph, and a large, framed photograph of an Italian chef she called Luigi. Two Boston terriers followed her everywhere. Shelly was a classy Italian lady who commanded respect, and I could see where Waylen got his good manners with women. It was nice to see where he came from, finally. His mom was kind and gracious, but I could tell she wasn't thrilled about me living there. It took time, but Waylen's mom and sister both came around. Eventually, they saw how devoted I was to Waylen and how happy we made each other.

One of the first things Waylen and I did was go to the north rim of the Grand Canyon, where we camped out in a secluded spot that Waylen had visited before. We had total privacy because only rock crawlers or off-road vehicles could get back there, and Waylen's truck was modified to navigate rough terrain. We parked near a ledge by a cluster of cottonwood and fir trees and erected the popup camper on the back of his truck. It was August, and the hot, dry wind wrapped itself around us, prodding us to take off our clothes. The canyon walls looked like melting lava that had cooled and frozen in time. Beyond, the mountains shone purple, red, and gold. The Colorado River glinted through the landscape at the bottom of the canyon.

As the sun dipped into the west, the sky seemed to burst into flames. Hawks soared across the clouds, calling to each other. The leaves around us rustled with unseen life. As the light softened and the temperature cooled, Waylen built a fire. I placed flat rocks on the hot embers and balanced a small cooking stove to heat soup. Once the sun sank, the sky lit up with millions of stars. The fire shot sparks high into the air and cast shadows that danced all around us. Alone, I would've been terrified. I shivered, and Waylen rubbed my arms, then got up to get a blanket from the truck, which he draped over my shoulders. He kept his arm around me until I felt warm again. We had sex by the fire and then again in the camper. We had sex whenever we weren't sitting around naked.

Our next stop was Utah's Zion National Park, where we spent a few days exploring trails, hiking the Narrows, and wading through the warm Virgin River surrounded by gorge walls that reached a thousand feet up. Then we were off to the Burning Man festival in the desert. It was Waylen's first time, and we had a blast. It was so different being at Burning Man with Waylen. He didn't hit on other women or complain about me like Blake did.

Back in Phoenix, Waylen and I lived at his mom's while I continued to travel to Vegas for work. But we were always planning our next adventure.

In September, we drove cross country to North Carolina, sleeping, cooking, and watching movies in the back of the white Silverado he called the Duramax. We even popped popcorn back there. At night, Waylen found a Planet Fitness or Walmart, where we parked overnight. He kept a Planet Fitness membership, so we could work out and shower before going to bed in the Duramax. I felt carefree at last.

Once in North Carolina, Waylen decided that we should go to California for the upcoming Wasteland Weekend, a Mad Max post-Apocalyptic festival. I reminded him that Blake was very involved with Wasteland Weekend, and that I'd promised him that we wouldn't show up together after the breakup. Waylen was disappointed and stayed quiet most of the drive back. I was angry at Blake for still trying to control us. Again and again, I apologized to Waylen. Finally, he assured me not to worry because he had an idea. We'd go to Wasteland, and Blake would never know.

"We'll be incognito," Waylen said. I had many questions, but he said, "Trust me."

Waylen took the doors off his electric Nissan Leaf, painted it camouflage, hung big chains to the rear doors, and mounted guns to the hood. Then we went to a Military Surplus store, bought a bunch of old clothing and fashioned it into Mad Max post-Apocalyptic outfits. We turned our sad situation into a fun preparation party. Waylen loaded the Leaf onto his trailer and hitched it to the Duramax. When we got to the campsite, we unloaded the Leaf and covered the Duramax with a tarp to hide it from Blake and his friends. People loved the Leaf. They said it was a perfect post-Apocalyptic vehicle because it was completely silent. Blake and his friends had no idea.

After our Wasteland trip, we went to Baja 1000, a one-thousand-mile off-road race for trophy vehicles. We traveled down the coast, exploring old mining towns, beaches, and museums. Sometimes we slept in the back of the Duramax right on the beach. The sound of crashing waves was relaxing, and the fresh ocean breeze felt healing. During those nights together, we began planning our new life in Phoenix.

# CHAPTER EIGHTEEN

We arrived back in Phoenix the day before Thanksgiving and spent the holiday with Waylen's mom. In December, Waylen started looking for a job and got hired as a Mechanical Engineer for a guy who imported Land Rovers. With Waylen's blessing, I started looking into strip clubs in Phoenix. Now that I was approaching forty, I wasn't sure I'd be able to compete with the twenty-somethings flooding the clubs. We visited a few clubs together, observing the dancers, patrons, management, and tip flow.

While living with Waylen's mom, I worked briefly at a club called Bliss, where I made decent money but wasn't satisfied. In January 2018, I went to Vegas to see clients one last time. Even though Waylen knew and said he was okay with it, I worried it would hurt our relationship. I knew it was the last time. I wanted a normal life free of guilt, and I was in love with Waylen.

While I was in Vegas, Waylen found a rental house, moved our stuff in, and sent pictures. It was an old farmhouse from the 1800s remodeled with modern interiors and appliances. It was gorgeous, and I couldn't wait to come home to him. We'd been at his mom's for over four months, and I was excited to finally have our own place. It was something I had dreamt of since leaving California.

After we moved, Waylen mentioned a club called Sugar 44 he passed by on his way to work that looked busy. He suggested I check it out, and I went to audition. Sugar 44 was a popular, upscale club that welcomed a variety of dancers. The oldest dancer was in her late fifties with a banging body and a slew of dedicated patrons. Another dancer proudly showed off her belly, seven months pregnant. Several more were in their forties. They hired me on the spot, and I started working that same night. I worked the day shift and made a lot of money there.

Waylen was secure enough with himself and our relationship that he didn't feel threatened by other men paying for my attention. He loved watching me dance and understood it was a job that paid well. Waylen said he didn't mind as long as I didn't see customers outside the club, fool around, or lie to him about anything. I intended to keep my promise. I didn't want to lose Waylen.

The allure of drugs began to fade as my relationship with Waylen grew stronger. The feeling I had with him was far more potent than any substance, even crack. With Waylen, I didn't want or need to escape. The present moment was enough. His lack of judgment allowed me to settle into the safety of being myself. Waylen had seen the wildest side of me and hadn't run away. If I did a little coke one night, he didn't get angry or walk away or make me feel ashamed. He simply said, "That's not good for you."

At a club one night, I did a line in the bathroom and sat next to him, playing with his hair. The drug rushed through me, exaggerating my senses. Waylen gently brushed my hand away from his head. "You're not yourself," he said.

"I am myself, just more excited."

"I like you the way you are without the drugs. That stuff will destroy your brain and body, and I'll miss them."

I was too high to argue with him, but it nagged me throughout the night. Waylen was right. He'd said these things before, that I could have a heart attack anytime and that I was risking the ability to have kids. After my ordeal with Blake, I'd started to put the idea of having kids behind me, but with Waylen, I was beginning to think differently about everything.

As summer arrived, I decided it was time to introduce my family to Waylen, so we flew to visit their new home in Iowa. I was nervous because we weren't married, and Waylen wasn't Amish. My mom glared at Waylen as he stood nervously by the door, and my dad looked him up and down, staring as he chewed on his pipe. Waylen squirmed under their gaze. I felt so bad for him. The little kids kept fighting over who got to sit next to us, and Waylen laughed and scooched over so they could take turns. I could tell that my parents and my brother and sister-in-law were uncomfortable. Waylen only spoke when he was asked a question. Mom took a handkerchief out of her pocket, sniffling as she wiped the tears from her eyes.

I knew that bringing my boyfriend to their house was against the Amish rules, and I felt bad for disrespecting them. Later, they pulled me aside and explained that it wasn't that they disliked Waylen, but we were breaking the Ordnung, which they reminded me laid out strict guidelines around courtship. "It's just not our way," my dad said.

Secretly, I hoped they'd be more accepting and open-minded than they used to be, but I told them I wouldn't bring him back to the house again until we were married. They thanked me for understanding.

While in Iowa, Waylen bought a cool RV and fixed it up. Instead of flying back to Arizona, we drove the RV back. The trip was one of our favorite adventures. We took our time and explored interesting places along the way.

Three weeks before my thirty-ninth birthday, Waylen and I went out to dinner with his mom at Oregano's, an Italian restaurant in Phoenix, and she asked me what I wanted to do for my birthday. I shrugged. "I don't know. It would be nice to spend it with Waylen and go out to dinner or something."

Waylen shook his head. "It's our second birthday as a couple. If you could do anything, what would it be?" His almond-shaped eyes met mine, challenging me while his mouth sported a teasing smile. Try me, his expression said.

I met his gaze, raising an eyebrow, signaling that I'd meet his challenge. "I've always wanted to go to Cuba."

Waylen's eyes widened as he nodded slowly. He was trying to look casual, but his smile gave him away. He was impressed.

"You said anything," I reminded him.

Cuba seemed so exotic to me. I'd seen pictures of Havana streets lined with those old cars from the 1950s. The storefronts in the background made it look as if the place was stuck in time, like the Amish, only different. Out of all my wildest dreams, Cuba seemed the most unattainable. I didn't think I'd ever actually go there. Or so I thought. Waylen had other plans, and for the next three days, he kept asking about it while looking up flights and hotels. At first, I thought he was just having fun, playing along with my fantasy. That night, he sat in front of the computer, looking intently at the screen. "These tickets are not expensive," he said. "I think we can do it. Between the two of us, it's possible." Within a few minutes, he'd bought the plane tickets and booked the rooms. I couldn't believe it. We were really going to Cuba!

We arrived in Havana on a Sunday afternoon. As soon as the airport doors slid open, the warm breeze enveloped us, and I felt as though I was stepping into another world. Waylen held my hand as we navigated the Spanish-speaking taxi drivers and found our way to the Airbnb, a small fifth-floor walkup near Old Havana Square.

We walked for hours that evening along the boulevards lined with palm trees and vintage cars. We stopped at a tiny, hole-in-the-wall restaurant where romantic music played as we ate pasta with lobster and did tequila shots. Afterward, we sat in the park — like any other couple in love in old Havana.

Tipsy on tequila and the tropical Cuban breezes, we stumbled back to our room, where Waylen got the old window air conditioner going. I found a bottle of white wine in the mini-fridge and brought it along with two glasses to the patio overlooking the city lights. Waylen and I stood in the moonlight on the balcony watching the locals hugging and kissing by the stone wall that bordered the ocean. The sound of crashing waves, the warm, humid summer breeze, and the scent of the salty ocean soothed my soul as I sipped the wine. I looked at Waylen and smiled. "It feels like everyone is in love here," I said.

Waylen leaned in and put his arms around me. "Well, I am definitely in love," he said. He turned to face me, and our lips pressed together. My heart fluttered as he pulled me closer, his breathing got heavier, and I inhaled the taste of wine on his tongue. He grabbed my hips and paused, looking into my eyes. "I love you so much, Naomi. You're the perfect woman for me."

His deep gaze and sincere voice brought tears of joy to my eyes.

"Aww, Waylen. I love you so much, too. But why? Why do you love me? For one thing, I'm ten years older than you."

"I love that about you. There's no drama; you're spontaneous, easy to get along with, and you don't try to control me."

"I'm so glad you feel that way." I put my hands on the back of his head, pulled him back to my lips, and pressed my body against his to assure him of my feelings. He gently guided me towards the bedroom with his hands firmly on my waist.

"Let's go," he whispered. Like a gentleman, he opened the door for me and gestured inside. "After you, beautiful lady."

I followed his lead, and soon we were on the bed, kissing like we couldn't get enough of each other. "Let's do 69!" he called out.

I eagerly spread my legs. "That's my favorite!"

We got undressed, and Waylen lay on the bed wearing his sexy red boxers. Teasing him, I straddled him and rubbed against his big bulge, waiting to be freed.

"You feel so good," he whispered, pulling me closer. He wiggled out of his boxers and helped me out of my red lace thong. Facing his legs, I lowered my mouth to his erection. His hands massaged my ass as he ate me out. Throwing my head back, I massaged his hard cock with my tongue. He let out a moan of pleasure as my tongue teased his tip before sliding his shaft into my mouth. He slid a finger inside me as his tongue got more intense.

"Oh, Waylen. It feels so good," I moaned. I pushed down on his mouth even more, and his cock grew bigger and harder as I slid my tongue up and down. Gently squeezing his balls with one hand, I swallowed his cock deep into my throat. He wiggled and pulled his hips back, trying not to cum, which only turned me on even more. My legs started quivering as I released him from my mouth.

"I'm cumming!" I moaned in relief.

Waylen ruffled my hair as I lay in his arms for a few minutes.

Then, "Are you ready for more?"

"Always," I smiled.

I stretched onto my hands and knees and arched my back as he mounted me from behind and covered my neck in sensuous kisses, stimulating my G-spot with every thrust. Our breathing intensified, and we let out a unified cry as we reached our peak.

Waylen had planned a surprise trip for the following day. He woke me up at sunrise, and we got into an old blue taxi van for a two-hour drive into the mountains. We were going horseback riding. Waylen had planned the whole thing because he knew how much I loved horses. We sat in the back behind three other couples for the rough ride through steep and windy roads. Every time we hit a bump, we bounced off the seat and laughed, grabbing ahold of each other.

We stopped in a magnificent valley dotted with steep limestone hillsoverlooking bright green fields of tobacco, fruits, and vegetables. The horses were all lined up and ready for us. Waylen and I began side by side; he held out his hand and I leaned in to reach it. We stayed interlocked for a few moments before my horse picked up his pace and pulled ahead. I tugged the reins, urging him to slow down, which only made him whinny and buck. The tour guide asked me not to hold him back because he used to be the lead horse and was accustomed to being in front. She was training another horse to be the lead but instructed me to let him walk ahead. I didn't want to be in front; I wanted to be with Waylen. But horses have a pecking order, and unfortunately, Waylen's horse was last, and the other horses wouldn't let him pass despite Waylen's best efforts. I kept looking back at Waylen, who just waved at me. Ignoring the guide's wishes, I tried to get my horse to stop so Waylen could catch up. He stomped his feet impatiently and nipped at the other horses as they passed, so I gave up trying to get to Waylen.

At that moment, I realized how badly I always wanted Waylen to be by my side. I relaxed in this sudden, blissful knowing as my horse carried me effortlessly through the steep winding trail through magnificent scenery. Was I dreaming? The emerald fields and mountains seemed never-ending. I began to enjoy being in the lead because nothing obstructed my view. For the first time in a long time, I felt at peace; I felt grounded. I imagined the blissful future I'd craved for so long. Life with Waylen felt right.

When I looked back again, I could no longer see him, but I could feel him, the permanence of him, and the promise that we'd each have a story to tell when we were side by side again.

When we returned to the starting point, Waylen dismounted and ran to me, wrapping his arms around me as if we'd been separated for days. Back together, we held hands during a boat tour through a maze of underground caves. We ended the day on a tobacco farm, where we split a cigar. Waylen showed me how to puff gently and not inhale the thick, sweet smoke.

The following night, we stayed in a castle built in the late 1800s overlooking the small city. Tall white pillars lined the winding staircases that wrapped around the old building. A small fountain bearing a naked statue greeted us in the courtyard. We continued through a tall doorway into a museum-like interior filled with antiques, and we stood there for a moment to absorb the beauty of it.

Our room continued the theme from downstairs with bedding, a headboard, a sofa, and drapes all made of matching reddish-brown velvet. I ran my hands over the comforter, enjoying its soft luxury. We stood on the balcony overlooking the city, breathing in the air, cool and fragrant from a quick afternoon rain shower. Then we ventured out to a nearby restaurant and ordered Pina Coladas and seafood and decided to find the strange-looking tower we saw from our balcony. We walked for what felt like forever, but I had Waylen by my side and the weather was magnificent. We strolled through the town, commenting on the architecture, old cars, and music trickling out from porches and windows.

The peak we'd seen was the steeple of a huge Catholic church. Waylen had grown up Catholic and so we went inside for Mass. It was nothing like the church in Amishland. The ceilings seemed impossibly high, and the light from outside shone through shiny stained glass windows depicting scenes from the bible. Although the Mass was conducted in Spanish, Waylen knew what to do, and I followed his lead.

Back in our room, as the sun set over the mountains, we opened a bottle of champagne to celebrate my birthday. Waylen suggested I take off my dress. "Let's take a shower," he whispered.

Water and suds slid down my breasts as Waylen massaged them. With his hands on my hips, he steered me to turn around and squeezed me close against him, rubbing the tip of his cock between my legs. I bent over trying to guide him deeper, but he resisted, still teasing me. I turned around, got on my knees, and gently pushed him against the shower wall. Water trickled down my face as I licked his cock from the base to the tip and squeezed his inner thighs. He guided his hard shaft into my mouth with his hands, and I slowly devoured him. "That feels so good, Naomi," he whispered.

He grew bigger and harder and let out a moan of relief as his cock pulsed inside my mouth. When I looked up at him, he was smiling. "I want to make you squirt," he said.

Excited for my turn, I grabbed some towels and laid them on the bed so I wouldn't make a mess. I spread out and tried to relax, stay present, and let go. Waylen ruffled my hair as he cradled my head in his arms. I pulled his head in and kissed his lips. The kissing got more intense, and he hopped on top of me. With one hand, he teased my nipples and with the other, he played with my clit, slipping two fingers inside. I arched my back, aroused, right on the edge of cumming. Waylen pulled back and increased the pressure on my G-spot with his fingers while sucking my clit. My breathing got heavier, and my moaning got louder as the pressure built. I felt like a volcano, ready to explode.

"I'm getting close," I whispered as my legs quivered. He slipped in another finger, and just like that, he hit the magic button. The floodgates opened. I let out a scream of relief as I squirted. He continued to suck on my clit and finger me as I squirted a bit more.

Euphoria engulfed my body, and I collapsed. Waylen kissed my forehead and ran his fingers through my hair. I felt like I was dreaming. The way he held and loved me was exactly how I imagined being in love would feel.

The next day was my birthday. We got up early and took another long bus ride along the beautiful ocean to Varadero — a touristy beach town. Waylen hailed a horse and carriage ride from the bus station to the resort. The all-inclusive hotel was within walking distance of the ocean and surrounded by tall palm trees bearing coconuts. I wanted to pick one so badly, but I wasn't tall enough. Waylen offered to let me stand on his shoulders to reach one, but I refused, not wanting to risk hurting his shoulder. We spent the afternoon drinking strawberry daiquiris and Pina Coladas in a private beachside cabana. In front of us, the water was clear blue and warm. Above us, the light clouds sheltered us from the sun. We swam all afternoon and built castles from the white sand.

I was sunbathing when I heard Waylen calling to me. "Naomi! I have a surprise for you."

Sitting up, I saw him standing with his arms stretched out like he wanted to hug me. As I walked closer, I could see he was surrounded by a big heart he'd drawn in the sand. Next to it, he'd written, "Love Forever — Waylen and Naomi."

He wrapped his arms around me and kissed me. My heart melted as he looked into my eyes. "I love you."

I squeezed him tight. "I love you, too, Waylen. This birthday's been everything I ever could've imagined and more." I kissed him again and again.

Walking back to our room, we saw a big coconut lying on the ground, and Waylen picked it up and handed it to me. "Looks like you got your coconut after all," he said, smiling. I was so excited to get a coconut, and it was delicious.

In the morning, we went out on a boat to go snorkeling. As soon as we jumped off the boat, I began to panic because of the big waves. Waylen noticed I was struggling and quickly came to assist me, holding my hand as the tour guide took pictures of us swimming with the fish. It was so different than being on vacation with Blake or anyone else. That day convinced me that if Waylen and I could have this much fun while traveling together, we could navigate life together, too. With Waylen, every day could be an adventure, and I wouldn't need to chase drugs to fill any voids. I'd found what I was looking for when I searched past that dangerous river bend. The treasure at its end was Waylen—and all I had to do was not mess it up.

Becoming a mother was something I'd secretly craved for a long time. That same year, I got pregnant but sadly miscarried at ten weeks, which devastated both Waylen and me. I went to an IVF doctor who performed many tests and concluded my chances of conceiving and delivering a baby were almost zero because of my age and the quality of my eggs. That didn't stop us from trying. Five months later, I tested positive again. But after only five days, I miscarried again. Then I had an epiphany. I was content with my life and having a kid might cramp my style. I made peace with the fact I'd never have a child. Waylen assured me he was also fine with not having kids. Little did we know the universe had a different path in store for us.

# CHAPTER NINETEEN

Some of my customers brought me gifts. It was part of the job, and Waylen was okay with that. One guy offered to buy my dance outfits, and Waylen said it was fine to meet him at the store to pick them out. When Diego, a short Mexican guy from California, asked what I wanted for Christmas in 2019, I thought about what we needed. In the past, Diego had bought me a bicycle for my birthday, and we'd met at the shop to pick it up.

I told Diego that I'd always wanted a down comforter. He was very excited and said I could pick out any comforter I wanted. There was only one problem. I hated malls and mall parking lots, so Diego suggested I meet him at his hotel to park, and he'd drive us there. Once we picked up the comforter from Macy's, it was still too early to go to work, so Diego took me to breakfast near his hotel. He never asked me to sleep with him; he was simply happy to be in my presence.

Around noon, he drove me back to the hotel parking lot. We sat in his car for a few minutes as I thanked him over and over for the comforter. I couldn't help feeling guilty, like I was taking advantage of him. Diego insisted that he just wanted to see me happy, but I couldn't help feeling like I owed him something. I gave him a hug and two quick pecks on the lips, grabbed the comforter, and drove to work. I didn't hear from Waylen all day, and if he replied at all, his tone was curt.

I had no idea Waylen was filming the whole thing in the parking lot. I'd told Waylen that I was going to meet a regular customer at Macy's. There was no reason to lie, but I thought he'd have a fit if I told him I'd parked at a hotel.

When I got home, Waylen was sitting at the table in the kitchen. He immediately started asking questions.

"Where did you go today?"

"I went to Macy's, bought the comforter, and went to work."

"Are you sure that's the only place you went?"

"Yes, why?"

"Where else did you go today?" That's when I realized he tracked my car's location.

"Okay, I met Diego at his hotel so he could drive."

"Do you kiss all your customers?"

"No, I don't kiss any of them."

"Are you sure?"

"Sometimes on the cheek but not on the lips."

Somehow, Waylen knew. "I may have pecked him on the lips as a thank you."

Waylen showed me the video on his phone. "It looks like more than two quick pecks," he said. "We're done. I'm breaking up with you."

I started to cry. "It didn't mean anything. I was just trying to be nice because I felt guilty."

Waylen wasn't swayed by my tears. "We're not getting married and I'm definitely not having kids with you."

I was heartbroken. And all over a comforter.

Waylen went into his computer room and shut the door. I called his mom, crying that I didn't cheat on her son, but that I was sorry. I felt like I failed myself. Was this the old me? I never wanted to be that person again. His mom told me to calm down and that Waylen would change his mind.

I knocked on the door to his computer room, then cracked it open. Waylen sat at the desk with his back to me. "I'm not talking to you," he said.

"I just wanted to tell you that you can sleep in the bed if you want."

He didn't respond, so I left but kept the door open. Eventually, he came to bed, but as promised, he wouldn't talk to me. I could barely sleep.

The next day, Waylen came home from work and said he'd posted our situation on Reddit, from a burner account after changing our identities.

"Everyone says you're a slut and that I should break up with you. The consensus is that you definitely cheated on me."

I thought it was so messed up that he went on Reddit to ask all those strangers what to do about our private life.

"People on Reddit are always right," he said, but he looked at me as if I could change his mind.

I couldn't imagine my life without him. Where would I go? What would I do? I couldn't believe it could all be gone in the blink of an eye. We continued talking over the next couple of days, and I begged and pleaded with him to give me another chance. We'd built such a strong foundation. "Please don't throw it away," I implored.

"I'm not the one throwing it away. You are."

I've learned it's better to tell the truth no matter how hard it is."

Finally, Waylen said, "We can stay together, but I'm not kissing you for a long time, and I'm not getting married for at least five years, so I can make sure you're not a cheater."

"Whatever you want!" I practically jumped into his arms. He finally believed me. Waylen pulled back a little and looked serious as he held my head in his hands.

"Naomi, you can't do drugs ever again. You could have a heart attack and die instantly. If you go back to using, we might not be able to have a child."

Relief rushed through me as I realized it never occurred to me to use when I thought I was losing Waylen. I didn't know until later how significant this was. More than a year and a half had passed since the last time I got high, and I was astonished. If I ever thought about drugs, it was quickly replaced by the possibility of having a family with Waylen, which felt much more important.

Right after the comforter incident, I sprained my ankle while camping. It took over two months for my ankle to fully recover, and after the boot came off, I had to go to physical therapy. In March, I went back to work for two days before the club shut down because of the pandemic. Waylen worked from home, and it was nice to be around him all the time. During the shutdown, we created our own little world and had a great time going for walks, watching TV, and cooking together. It was another reminder of how compatible we are. And I got to ride my bicycle almost every day. It was nice to focus on my health and well-being when everything felt uncertain and strange. I lost fifteen pounds and looked amazing. I also did a lot of coloring to pass my time. Life finally felt balanced, the way I'd imagined English life would be with the perfect partner by my side, able to watch TV or listen to music and ride my bicycle whenever I wanted.

Two months later, the club reopened and everyone had to wear a mask. I didn't mind because it meant I could wear less makeup, although some customers asked me to remove the mask while I danced for them in the VIP room. They said they wanted "to see my pretty face," but I didn't budge. After six weeks, the pandemic got worse, and the club shut down again. Happily, I continued to enjoy the tranquility of my private life with Waylen again.

A few weeks later, I got a surprise positive pregnancy test on my mom's birthday. I sat on the toilet, silently staring at the results, not knowing if I should cry tears of joy or sadness. I wanted to feel hopeful, but after two miscarriages, I felt scared. Should I run to Waylen and show him, or wait a few days to see what happened? Although torn, I decided to stay optimistic. Waylen was working in his computer room when I stuck my head in and said, "I have a surprise for you."

He casually turned around. "Yeah, what is it?"

With my hands behind my back, I walked closer. "Guess," I said.

He tried to look, but I wouldn't let him see. "I have no idea," he said. I couldn't wait any longer and held up the test. Smiling, he jumped up and hugged me. "That's awesome," he whispered then we laughed and cried, still holding each other.

"This is the one," I told him. "The baby I'll carry to term and deliver."

Waylen turned on our favorite music, took my hand, twirled me around, and we danced in the computer room. We were so elated that the universe gave us another chance to become parents.

# EPILOGUE

The first twelve weeks of my pregnancy were filled with worries and doctor appointments. Every day, I prayed for a healthy pregnancy and baby. Thankfully, the genetic and other tests indicated that we were both fine. As the pregnancy moved along, I started to relax and enjoy it. Every day, I wondered if we'd be blessed with a boy or a girl, and not knowing was exciting because we'd be happy either way. I wondered about the baby's eyes and hair color and who they would resemble. What personality would they have?

My tiny little dancer stretched and moved a lot, especially at night. Sometimes it felt like the baby was doing somersaults or trying to run. My stomach jolted with every move, startling me. For the most part, I loved being pregnant; it was an exhilarating experience. Waylen and I bought two acres of property outside the city to prepare for our family. We already had chickens, and after the baby came and we got settled, we planned on getting more animals for our little ranch. This was something I'd dreamt of for a long time.

Since I stayed home during my pregnancy, I decided to crochet and sew blankets for the baby, but the idea of sewing was overwhelming because I hadn't done it in so long. Blake had given me a little sewing machine for Christmas one year, and I'd only used it once or twice in the five years since. I pulled it out of storage, dusted it off, and discovered it didn't work. I felt so disappointed in this crappy little sewing machine, and it brought back so many memories and emotions of my relationship with Blake. I decided to sew it by hand instead. It wasn't ideal, but I could do it. Halfway through and frustrated, I took one last look at the sewing machine. I tightened the needle and adjusted the tension, and suddenly it came to life. I couldn't believe it. The sewing machine wasn't crappy after all; it just wasn't adjusted correctly. Grateful, I sewed the blanket with the sewing machine.

It wasn't long before the blanket was complete, and I held it up for Waylen, who said it was the most beautiful blanket he'd ever seen. I knew that wasn't true, but I thought my mother would be proud, and I felt proud, too.

In March 2021, I gave birth to a girl. We named her Stormy. Actually, I named her Stormy. Waylen thought it sounded like a stripper name, but eventually, he gave in. Our lives changed dramatically when we became parents, and our beautiful daughter brought us even closer. Being a mother is the hardest but most rewarding job, and it's by far my favorite chapter in life, although it's exhausting at times. Sometimes I miss the free time I had before Stormy came into our lives, but I wouldn't trade motherhood for anything. Our daughter truly is a blessing. She is so smart and calm and has such a fun personality.

In August of 2021, when Stormy was almost six months old, I flew to Iowa to introduce her to my Amish family. I felt uneasy not knowing how they would react to her in her English clothes, but I hoped they would accept her. When I pulled into their driveway, I saw Dad working in his buggy shop. He peered out the window and a smile crossed his face as I pulled Stormy from the car. My brother's young kids came running and grinning from all directions to greet us, and shyly asked, "*Wie geht's* (How's it going)?"

"We're doing good," I said as I walked towards the house. Dad came out of the buggy shop to greet us. He took a puff from his pipe and said, "Well, who is this?"

I stopped and said, "This is little Stormy."

He reached out, touched her hand, and cooed to her in a gentle voice. Stormy smiled and babbled as they had their first conversation. I hadn't seen my dad smile like that in a long time—and I felt relieved that he was happy to meet his new granddaughter, even though she wasn't Amish.

Mom stood inside the screen door, smiling as I approached the porch, and opened the door. "This must be Stormy." Stormy got excited and started flapping her arms as Mom talked to her.

I smiled and said yes, then Mom reached for her and Stormy willingly went into her arms. Jokingly, Mom said, "I can see she gets plenty to eat."

"It must be all the good mother's milk she drinks," I teased back. I could see the joy in her eyes as she played with Stormy.

My sister and I dressed Stormy in a little Amish dress and *kapp*, and she looked adorable. I could tell that Mom and Dad were delighted to see her dressed Amish. Mom playfully said, "See, she already has Amish clothes to wear if you decide to stay." I nodded my head so as not to hurt her feelings.

I was grateful that everyone accepted my daughter, and just as I expected, my nieces named their dolls Stormy. They enjoyed playing with her and bickered over who got to hold her.

Mom gave me an Amish dress, two homemade beaded bracelets, and a little book to take home for Stormy's first birthday. Moments like those remind me how much my relationship with my mother has grown, and I felt closer to her than ever before. I wanted her to know her granddaughter.

Almost a year later, we went to visit my parents again. Stormy was fifteen months old, walking, talking, and playing peek-a-boo. She'd learned the song, "If You're Happy and You Know It Clap Your Hands," and danced around the house, clapping her hands and stomping her feet. This time, we walked right into the house where Mom was cooking lunch. I put Stormy down and sang the song for her, eager to show her off, and sure enough, Stormy danced and clapped and babbled along. Then Mom turned around and started singing the song, too, even clapping her hands and stomping her feet. It was so moving to see Mom and Stormy interacting this way, especially since I'd never known my mom to listen to music or dance in her life.

When lunch was ready, Mom called out to Dad in the buggy shop. I watched him walk up the porch steps and notice Stormy standing inside the screen door. He covered his face, then popped his hands open. "Peek-a-boo!"

Stormy giggled and repeated, "Peek-a-boo." Then she hid behind the door and their game continued inside the house. Dad hid behind furniture while she screeched and chased him. When she caught him, he swung her onto his lap and bounced her on his knee. It was so beautiful to watch them play together. Dad still didn't say much to me, but I saw tears roll down his cheeks, and I couldn't help but wonder if they were tears of joy, unlike before. I'll likely never ask. It's an unspoken agreement between us that I'm to respect the boundaries he's built between us, and I've learned it's his right not to stray from the path of safety he's chosen. I've accepted the fact that I'll never have a close relationship with my father. I wished I could record the moments of my parents singing and dancing and playing with Stormy, but that's forbidden. Instead, I'll always cherish those memories and relay them to Stormy when she's older.

Looking back, I enjoyed my childhood and feel proud that I was Amish. Being raised on the path of God gave me a peaceful and spiritual childhood. I knew I was loved even though my parents never said, "I love you." They showed me love with their actions instead of words. I'm so grateful for my parents and all they taught me. They gave me a strong foundation that I can always rely on, and they still loved and accepted me even after I left the Amish.

Life as a drug addict and a prostitute felt carefree at times, but it was also incredibly traumatizing and hard on my soul. I'm on a healing journey and had to learn how to love myself again. Feeling loved and accepted by Waylen and his family helped me love and believe in myself again. I feel incredibly fortunate that I was able to overcome my addiction and that I didn't die from an overdose. Breaking the habit took a lot of willpower and strength that I often didn't think I had. I had to dig deep and ask myself what path I truly wanted to follow. The sturdy foundation I had from growing up Amish helped me to eventually rediscover my strength and put me back on the right path. It wasn't easy, but I'm glad I chose sobriety. The quality of my life and health gradually improved. Every day, I wake up and feel grateful I get to live another day when before I often wished my life would end. Today, I don't need drugs to escape life; I choose to live in the present. Being sober has been exhilarating.

I met many women throughout my life, especially when I was dancing, but only a few became close friends. Being in a relationship was always my priority. When one relationship ended, I found another one right away. I never liked being alone because I came from such a big family, so my relationships were dysfunctional. I was insecure, dishonest, and jealous, but I learned valuable lessons from each of them.

I've matured and grown in so many ways. Waylen and I continue to have a healthy relationship and support each other no matter what. Our trust, communication, and respect for each other are stronger than ever. My relationship with Waylen differs from all my other relationships because I chose to be honest with him about who I was from the beginning. I feel empowered by my honesty and don't need to prove myself to him. Waylen allows me to be myself. Open communication and trust are the foundations of our relationship, and I never worry that he will cheat on me. I feel secure with who he is and trust him completely. Life has been so peaceful with a loving, trusting partner. I've learned there will be disagreements in any relationship and that it's okay. It's so important to trust the process and lead with love instead of jealousy.

I love my family. Waylen and Stormy are my whole heart and world. While I respect many of the values my parents instilled in me, I want to raise my daughter differently. I want to have a good relationship with her based on open and honest communication about the world we live in, including its darker paths, so hopefully, she doesn't choose the same paths I did.

I believe I made certain decisions because I wasn't educated about sex and drugs. My family tried to hide the existence of both, which just made me more curious. Anytime I discovered a new drug, I wanted to know how it felt. I enjoyed having sex, and it was an easy way to support my drug habit. Sex and drugs seemed extremely taboo, but that's what my rebellious side wanted to experience. I danced most of my adult life, twenty-one years total. Dancing gave me a tremendous amount of freedom which my spirit craves. It allowed me to live a unique lifestyle and do everything I wanted.

Perhaps most importantly, I love the person I've become. My life has been an adventure. If I could go back and change anything, I would have said no to drugs, and I would've stayed in college and pursued a career as an accountant. Yet I recognize that the paths I chose and every experience I've had all led me to the person I am and the life I have now.

Today, the river is calm despite the chaos and exhaustion that come with being a mom. When the current moves too quickly, I can hold on to Waylen and catch my breath. It's so much easier now. Even though I know the terrain might get rocky, I'm confident that Waylen and I can navigate it together. We'll teach Stormy how to swim in calm and rough waters and how to approach the scariest bends in the river. We'll tell her the story of her Amish grandparents and her non-Amish families, and how we fell in love against all odds. And maybe one day, I will tell her the story of my amazing adventures as an Amish stripper.

# ACKNOWLEDGMENTS

First, I'm so grateful for my partner and our daughter. You've both been so patient and given me the time I needed to pursue my dream to publish this book. You give me purpose each and every day. I love and appreciate you so much. Also, a very special thank you to my partner and his family for accepting me, allowing me to be myself, and always being supportive of me and the choices I make.

I'm so thankful for my Amish parents, my four sisters, and seven brothers. I think of you every day and feel blessed that you still accept me, even though I chose a different lifestyle. I'm grateful for all the values you instilled in me as a child to have a strong foundation as an adult.

I'm especially thankful for my BFF soul sister for life, Sarah Hershberger, with whom I connected shortly after I left the Amish. Sarah, you're always there for me, and continue to inspire and support me no matter how long it's been since our last phone call or visit.

Sincere gratitude to M. Maeve Eagan, my writing coach and editor, who encouraged me to explore the erotic side of my story, as well as some of its darker dynamics, and helped write sex scenes, dialogue, and prose to bring my memoir to life. Thank you for honoring my voice and for your invaluable guidance and support through the writing and publishing process.

A special thank you to Dr. Mike and Dr. Mary—my biggest cheerleaders for years. I appreciate your support and encouragement.

Sincere gratitude to my Beta readers, Sarah Hershberger and Dr. Mary. Your feedback was valuable and appreciated.

A big shoutout to the designers at TreeHouse Studio for coming through at the last minute and acing the cover and interior concept of my book.

Thank you to Karyn Kloumann at Nauset Press for line editing assistance.

Much appreciation to Randy, who believed in me when I didn't believe in myself and for taking me to Las Vegas, which gave me another shot at life.

Many thanks to Steve Chelski for providing some of the photos of me on the pole.

Last but not least, a big thank you to everyone who's helped and supported me along the way and made the transition from Amishland to my English life easier. I appreciate each and every one of you.

# ABOUT THE AUTHOR

Naomi Swartzentruber was raised in a strict religious community called the Swartzentruber Amish in Gladwin, Michigan. At seventeen, she ran away to live life among the English, got her GED, and took college classes before receiving her licenses in phlebotomy, medical assistance, and x-ray technician. After moving to Las Vegas, Naomi continued a career in exotic dancing for more than twenty years. She lives with her partner and daughter in Arizona where she enjoys gardening, raising chickens, and outdoor adventures with her family.

Website: examishgirl.com
TikTok: @amishinspiration
Instagram: @amishinspiration

Printed in Great Britain
by Amazon

36037149R00136